✳ PRAISE FOR *GRACE: A MODEL FOR GRIEVING*

T0279158

"The 'GRACE Grief Model' is a masterpiece that offers a new perspective on grief by blending well-known, evidence-based therapeutic theories into a singular model. *GRACE: A Model for Grieving* is groundbreaking, compressible, and shines a light on the human experience of grief. Anyone who has experienced loss or who works with individuals who are experiencing loss will find this book to be an invaluable resource."

—Rayan Al Jurdi, MD

"With straightforward language accessible to clinicians and clients, *GRACE: A Model for Grieving* provides practical exercises to change the relationship between self and grief. Dr. Kay Towns has given practitioners the gift of a stepwise approach to addressing the overlooked aspects of culture and spirituality in the treatment of grief."

—Dawn Ellison, DPC, LPC, former director of Doctor of Professional Counseling Program, Mississippi College

"These practical techniques provide the grieving individual the needed steps to create hope in their life when dealing with devastating loss. *GRACE: A Model for Grieving* is a go-to grief handbook for the bereaved, licensed mental health practitioners, and clergy and spiritual leaders."

—Rev. Jerry L. Terrill DSM, LPC-S, LMFT-S

"*GRACE: A Model for Grieving* is a gift to anyone on the journey of grief. The comprehensive model offers five practical tools to create insight and healing. Each person's unique and individual experience of grief is treated holistically, offering a pathway of growth through loss."

—Dr. Lorna Bradley, author of *Special Needs Parenting*

GRACE:
A Model for Grieving

Workbook

GRACE:
A Model for Grieving

Workbook

A Five-Step Guide for
Healing After Loss

KAY TOWNS, DPC, LPC

Hatherleigh Press is committed to preserving
and protecting the natural resources of the earth.
Environmentally responsible and sustainable practices
are embraced within the company's mission statement.

Visit us at hatherleighpress.com and register online
for free offers, discounts, special events, and more.

GRACE: A MODEL FOR GRIEVING WORKBOOK

Library of Congress Cataloging-in-Publication Data is available.
ISBN: 978-1-961293-05-2

Printed in the United States
10 9 8 7 6 5 4 3 2 1

This book is dedicated to my brother Blaine and sister Holly.

Loss may have shaped us but loss has not defined us.

Instead of being diminished by loss, you grow

stronger and more full of grace,

pouring yourself out as blessing to others.

✳ CONTENTS

❋ AUTHOR'S NOTE

FROM THE DEATH OF a loved one, to losing a job, to the rupture of a relationship, losses are an inevitable part of the human condition. Life's difficulties will always include losses—big and small—and loss remains part of every person's life story. At times, our losses may feel overwhelming, and the resulting individual and communal mental distress exacts a heavy toll personally and collectively. We could all benefit from additional healthy resources targeted to address loss and the accompanying grief that follows. I am grateful to be able to offer a new type of hope needed by many in the form of a novel evidenced-based approach to grief and loss—the GRACE Grief Model.

Within the grief process is an invitation to repair and heal. In its severe form, grief is called prolonged grief (formerly known as complicated grief), resulting when the difficult emotions of loss are severe and do not improve over time. Prolonged grief has made its way into the Diagnostic and Statistical Manual of Mental Disorders[1] as Persistent Complex Bereavement Disorder (PCBD) and has been deemed a health hazard with potentially life-threating implications. Further, Prolonged Grief Disorder (PGD) has also been identified in the DSM-5-TR.[2]

Current grief-related diagnoses and treatment models have been found to be lacking, including cognitive behavior therapy (CBT) which is presently recognized as the most efficacious model for grief treatment. CBT for the treatment of grief and prolonged grief has been aimed primarily at reducing symptomology. However, literature suggests CBT alone offers incomplete treatment for many who struggle with grief. This has been further detailed in my book, *GRACE: A Model for Grieving*, which is the complementary handbook to this workbook.

I created the GRACE Grief Model out of necessity. As an ordained United Methodist minister (order of deacon) and Licensed Professional Counselor, my work with others often centers on loss. In my prior grief work with clients and patients, I tried without success to find an evidenced-based model of grief that supports a person's personal individualized journey while also incorporating spirituality. It is from my need to find a more comprehensive grief model in hopes of better helping

---

1 American Psychiatric Association, 2013
2 American Psychiatric Association, 2022

xii   GRACE: A MODEL FOR GRIEVING WORKBOOK

others through their loss that my passion developed to create a novel approach to grief work, giving birth to the GRACE Grief Model.

In this new model, the restorative gift of grief is highlighted and affirmed. At its core, the GRACE Grief Model promotes healthy grieving and offers a powerful, evidenced-based opportunity to help grow and heal through loss recovery and restoration, including constructing meaning from our loss as we move forward in our grief process. The GRACE Grief Model presents grief as a gift and reparative renewal as the process through which regeneration and growth begin. Within the grief process is an invitation to repair from loss and heal loss wounds. Scripture reminds us that God does not allow pain without allowing something new to be born.[3] The reparative process of grieving enables this new growth and invites us to develop new and healthier ways of thinking, feeling, and behaving. Through this model, adaptive grief work invites cathartic constructivism (catharsis based on an individual's own experiences) for effectual healing.

The GRACE Grief Model uses elements of CBT along with elements of narrative therapy within a framework that supports individual beliefs, goals, and sense of purpose (meaning making inclusive of spirituality). My goal in creating this model is to offer an alternative grief treatment aimed at facilitating the grieving process and expanding grief treatment options to help more people. I was elated to observe the effectiveness of the GRACE Grief Model first-hand. As I worked in the hospital setting and in private practice, I found incorporating aspects of the GRACE Grief Model into individual and group therapies successfully supported patient healing from loss, even for patients stalled in their grieving process or struggling with prolonged grief. Within my practice, I regularly witness how the GRACE Grief Model provides a new system of support that other grief models lack, helping me more effectively treat and reach a broader and more diverse population.

Prior to the creation of the GRACE Grief Model, many existing grief models included CBT and CBT-based approaches, and also narrative therapy and narrative-based approaches. However, I was unable to locate a model that integrated CBT and narrative therapy within a meaning-making framework supporting individual beliefs, goals, and sense of purpose. The GRACE Grief Model achieves this and promotes a model of grief work that is biologically imperative, emotionally healing, and spiritualty nurturing.

Of note, while I have my own personal beliefs and ways of relating to the Divine, my religious views are not highlighted in this workbook, given the purpose of this text is to provide grief support to a broad population and, in doing so, value the uniqueness of each person's personal spiritual journey. I acknowledge here that because of my faith education and spiritual formation, many of the examples and illustrations I pull from and offer in this text do at times lean towards a Christian

---

3 Jeremiah 66:9

perspective. My intent is not to be exclusive or to alienate anyone with different religious or spiritual understandings.

Again, this book is intended for people who have been struggling with grief, and specifically is a complementary resource for those who are in grief counseling. This book is also intended for grief educators, psychotherapists, and other mental healthcare professionals.

The combined works of the *GRACE: A Model for Grieving* handbook and this book, *GRACE: A Model for Grieving Workbook*, reflect many years of personal and professional dedication towards helping people grieve in healthier ways. I sincerely hope you find this book and the GRACE Grief Model helpful as you move through your own grief journey.

—Dr. Kay Towns

HOW TO USE THIS WORKBOOK

THIS WORKBOOK IS AN accompaniment to the handbook *GRACE: A Model for Grieving*[4] and is intended for use by people who are struggling with grief, including prolonged grief. This workbook and the aforementioned *GRACE: A Model for Grieving* serve as helpful resources for patients and clients in grief counseling and are useful guides for grief educators, psychotherapists, psychiatrists, and other mental healthcare workers.

ABOUT THE CONTENTS

Within each chapter of this workbook are carefully selected and thoughtfully crafted exercises, tools, and techniques that support an adaptive (healthy) grief process using the GRACE Grief Model. These exercises, tools, and techniques have been researched and support an evidenced-based approach to grief work (see pages 19–24 for details). To make this material easier for your use, both the GRACE grief handbook and GRACE grief workbook (this book) align by chapter to facilitate you working through both books concurrently.

In this workbook you will find:

- **Chapters 1–2:** The first chapters provide an overview of grief and the GRACE Grief Model with supportive worksheets designed to help you better understand your grief.
- **Chapters 3–7:** These five chapters highlight the GRACE model's five-step process for grieving and offer exercises targeted at supporting the grief process. These chapters showcase each element of the GRACE Grief Model, providing you a new way to heal from loss.
- **Chapter 8:** This final chapter extends support for how to move forward with the "new normal" as you heal from loss. This chapter provides useful exercises, including a Loss-Recovery Remembering & Celebration Event.

---

4 Towns, 2024

GRIEF MAP GRAPHICS

The GRACE Grief Map (see page 6) uses the following graphics to help illustrate its six key components. You will also notice these graphics appear with corresponding exercises provided throughout this workbook.

 #1. World View

 #2. Loss View

 #3. Unhealthy Meaning (misalignment)

 #4. Stop, Pause, and Reflect

 #5. Search & Construct

 #6. New Healthy Meaning (alignment)

You may notice that some of the explanatory information provided in this workbook is also included in the *GRACE: A Model for Grieving* handbook. This repetition is intentional and serves two purposes: it is both an aid for those experiencing difficulty with concentration, memory, and/or distraction (common for persons struggling with grief), and also it offers essential core information from the *GRACE: A Model for Grieving* handbook in the event you, the reader, do not have access to the handbook. Please note that both books—*GRACE: A Model for Grieving* and *GRACE: A Model for Grieving Workbook*—are designed to be used together.

HELPFUL MODIFICATIONS

Because grief can make learning more difficult by impacting, for example, concentration, memory, and distractibility. The exercises provided in this workbook are designed to be easy to follow and also adaptable. Supportive adaptive modifications you may choose to utilize include changing the order of an exercise (the exercises do not necessarily need to be completed in sequential order), and changing the length of an exercise (as guided by your mental health professional, you may find that not all components of every exercise must be completed to achieve beneficial results). You are encouraged to work through the exercises, tools, and techniques with a support partner as appropriate (e.g., psychotherapist or other mental healthcare professional).

Disclaimers

In this book, only personal stories about me and my family are factual; all other stories and names in this work are fictional representations (scenarios) intended to represent actual cases for informational and illustration purposes. My decision not to include my clients'/patients' stories was made out of an abundance of caution to protect client/patient identities and their information. Any potential similarity in these scenario stories to real life are purely coincidental and are not based on any actual persons. I also note here, I was trained as a counselor in the hospital setting and subsequently practiced counseling professionally in a medical setting. Therefore, I often use the term "patient" rather than client to refer to those whom I have counseled and those I currently counsel.

 Chapter 1

ABOUT GRIEF

Topic: Understanding Grief

Exercises & Tools

- My Grief Type
- My Grief's Impact
- Drawing My Grief Symptoms
- Yearning and Searching
- My Personal Grief Model

WHAT IS GRIEF?

While loss refers to an *event* (death, divorce, illness, job layoff, etc.), grief is our *reaction* to that loss event. Simply put, grief is "the emotion of loss"[5] and affects a person's cognitive (thoughts), emotional (feelings), and behavioral (actions) responses.[6] Grief is a normal and essential part of our existence ingrained within our DNA as an ongoing mechanism for managing life's losses in ways that aim to promote healing. Grief is also a form of learning.[7] Advances in neuroscience help us better envision and understand grief and provide opportunities to reimagine existing mental health theories in light of new scientific findings. For example, in combining neuroscience with

---

5 Scheff, 2015, p. 458

6 Shear, 2011

7 O'Connor & Seeley, 2022

attachment theory, we learn that grief teaches us how to live in a world without that which we yearn for due to loss.[8]

The process of grieving, and especially learning to grieve in healthy ways, not only makes us feel better, it is essential and primary for our human survival.[9] The work of grief is an ongoing cycle that, like waves, will continue to ebb and flow in and out of our lives without a final ending. Of note, there is a distinction between ongoing adaptive (healthy) grief work and grief that is maladaptive, prolonged or severe (unhealthy). The GRACE Grief Model supports healthy ongoing grief work while helping address unhealthy grieving, including prolonged grief. In the GRACE Grief Model, grief is redefined as biologically imperative, emotionally healing, and spiritually nurturing.

GRIEF TYPES

There are many different types of grief. The types we will discuss here are normal grief, prolonged grief (formerly known as complicated grief), anticipatory grief, disenfranchised grief, abstract grief, and ambiguous grief. Of note, grief types can be overlapping. For example, the nature of ambiguous grief (ongoing loss that lacks closure) can often result in accompanying disenfranchised grief (unsupported and minimized loss).

Normal Grief (Integrated Grief)

Normal grief is healthy and part of the common human condition. Normal grief differs from abnormal (prolonged or complicated) grief in that "normal grief progresses from acute to integrated grief."[10] This normal progression entails moving from an acute state, marked by mental and emotional anguish, repeated thoughts of the loss, and neglect of routine life functioning, towards a healthy integration of grief signaled by acceptance of the loss, a reduction in mental and emotional suffering, and a return to a normalized life.

Prolonged Grief (Complicated Grief)

What happens when the natural flow of the grief process is disrupted? Interference in a healthy grief process could herald the onset of prolonged grief. While the majority of people's grief response will be "normal" and move them out of woundedness into a place of healthy healing after a loss event, for some the reaction to loss can be abnormal. Abnormal reactions of grief or complicated grief result from an obstruction of the path to integrated grief, causing profound and incessant distress

---

8 O'Connor & Seeley, 2022

9 Peña-Vargas, Armaiz-Pena, Castro-Figueroa, 2021

10 Moayedoddin & Markowitz, 2015, p. 364

pertaining to the loss.[11] Prolonged or complicated grief is an unhealthy grief response requiring diagnosis by a mental health professional. A diagnosis of prolonged grief is based on grief severity and duration and, if not treated, can cause long-term psychological problems. Of note, diagnostic criteria in the DSM-5-TR for Prolonged Grief Disorder (PGD) is limited to individuals struggling with bereavement.[12] Prolonged grief signals the normal process of healing has been derailed.[13] Statistics indicate that the approximate number of persons struggling with complicated grief is at least 7% in bereaved populations and 4% in general populations.[14]

If not treated, complicated grief is a general health hazard[15] and viewed as a potentially life-threatening condition.[16] Persons with complicated grief are at increased risk for co-existing mental and physical conditions, which includes higher risk of death, cancer, cardiovascular trouble, high blood pressure, suicidality, eating problems/disorders,[17] and depression.[18] Post-Traumatic Stress Disorder (PTSD) is also understood as a side effect of complicated grief.[19] Complicated grief symptoms include rumination, inability to make sense of the loss, catastrophic thinking, and avoidance, and is associated with prolonged distress, suicidality, and negative health.[20]

Anticipatory Grief

Another common type of grief response is anticipatory grief, which is understood as grief that occurs prior to a loss, as distinguished from grief occurring at or after a loss.[21] How can you have grief over a loss that has not happened? This type of grief can actually be fairly common and occurs when we believe correctly or incorrectly that a loss is likely or is going to happen. Examples include concerns that a company's cost-reductions will result in layoffs, escalation of fighting and hurt feelings between couples causing one partner to assume the relationship is ending, seeing a grandmother's illness progress and sensing she may not live much longer.

---

11 Shear, 2011; Simon, 2013

12 American Psychiatric Association, 2022

13 Shear, 2011

14 Enez, 2018; Kersting, Brahler, Glaesmer, & Wagner, 2011; Rosner, Pfoh, & Kotoucova, 2011

15 Miyabayashi & Yasuda, 2007; Nakajima, 2018

16 Shear et al., 2011

17 Ito et al., 2012

18 Simon, 2013

19 Linde, Treml, Steinig, Nagl, & Kersting, 2017

20 Shear, 2011

21 Hamilton, 2016

Disenfranchised Grief

In some cases, grief feels as if it cannot be openly or publicly acknowledged, socially supported, or publicly mourned, which is referred to as disenfranchised grief.[22] These types of losses are mostly unsupported. When I worked caring for the elderly in one of my church roles, I often heard these types of losses referred to as "non-casserole" events, meaning the parishioners and others never or rarely brought meals or other offers of support to those struggling with disenfranchised grief. Common examples of disenfranchised grief include LGBTQ+ issues, pregnancy losses, affairs, estrangements, pet losses, disabilities, etc.

Grief Caused by Abstract Loss

We universally recognize that loss includes physical losses, like the loss of people, animals, and things. These types of losses are tangible and more easily understood by most. However, not every loss is tangible or easily understood. Loss can also include the abstract, such as loss of one's beliefs, loss of love, loss of dreams and hopes, loss of independence, loss of ideations, etc. These types of non-tangible losses are abstract loss.

Ambiguous Grief

Ambiguous loss involves no closure in which "a situation of unclear loss that remains unverified and thus without resolution."[23] Ambiguous losses may go unrecognized, which can result in disenfranchisement. Ambiguous losses refer to the physical or psychological experiences that are not concrete[24] and can either be tangible (e.g., loss of a person, animal, or thing) or intangible (e.g., lost relationship, lost love, missing persons, and military deployment). The ambiguous loss cycle is never ending and rarely closes, resulting in a prolonged loss experience.[25]

---

22 Doka, 1989; Lathrop, 2017

23 Boss, 2016, p. 270

24 Betz & Thorngren, 2006

25 Betz & Thorngren, 2006

In this chapter's upcoming exercises, you will notice these two graphics at the top of each page:

Loss View

Stop, Pause, Reflect

The GRACE Grief Map has a total of six elements, each with a focused set of objectives to work through. Each of the elements also has a corresponding graphic.

These graphics indicate two (out of six) of the Grief Map elements: "Loss View" and "Stop, Pause, Reflect." The GRACE Grief Map is provided for you on the next page (note: the GRACE Grief Map is explained in more detail in the handbook *GRACE: A Model for Grieving*). In this chapter's exercises, "Loss View" and "Stop, Pause, Reflect" are the focus of each exercise. "Loss View" indicates a focus on the meaning you give to a specific loss, how you make sense of it, and "Stop, Pause, Reflect" steps us towards creating a new healthier understanding and meaning of loss. The remaining four elements, which you will learn about in the next chapter, are: World View, Unhealthy Meaning (misalignment), Search & Construct, and New Healthy Meaning (alignment). The GRACE Grief Map and each of its six corresponding graphics will be explained fully in the next chapter (pages 25–26). In this workbook's subsequent chapters, every exercise will include one or more of the six graphics as a reminder of which grief map element you are working through.

GRACE Grief Model: Grief Map*

Each exercise in this workbook includes elements of the GRACE Grief Map, while the Graphics Key (below) will highlight for you the corresponding area of focus and help you to identify progression along your Grief Map journey.

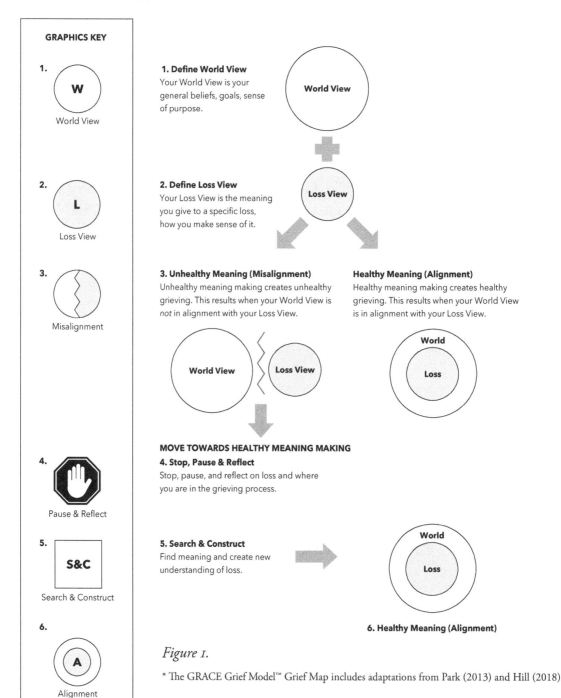

Figure 1.

* The GRACE Grief Model™ Grief Map includes adaptations from Park (2013) and Hill (2018)

EXERCISE: MY GRIEF TYPE

What type (or types) of grief are you experiencing (normal, prolonged, anticipatory, disenfranchised, abstract, ambiguous)?

Thinking about the type/types of grief you have just described for yourself, why do you believe you identify with this type of grief?

Example: Rory's Grief Type

Rory was always proud of his sister, and especially so when she enlisted to serve in the military. One late night, Rory awoke to dire news: his sister, who had been overseas on active duty and called out on a mission, never returned to base. After exhaustive searches, his sister remained missing and was presumed dead.

For Rory and his family, this loss was heart-wrenching. To compound their sorrows, there was no opportunity for closure; so many questions without answers, a funeral without a body. In this case, Rory was experiencing ambiguous grief (an ongoing loss that lacks closure).

GRIEF'S IMPACTS

Grief, as we have been learning, can impact us in many ways. So far, we have seen that grief affects us physically and mentally and we know grief's impacts can be felt individually and collectively. Grief's effect on us can also include the following:

Avoidant Behaviors. Actions you may take to escape from difficult thoughts and feelings. Sometimes we avoid by what we do (e.g., over-work instead of dealing with our painful feelings of loss) or what we do not do (e.g., avoid driving by the area where the death of a loved one occurred). While it is important to remember that each person's grief process, including how and when they grieve, may differ, avoiding the grief process can be problematic. Avoidance is different than healthy distractions that can be necessary and much needed breaks along the grief journey (e.g., taking time out from grief work to have dinner with friends). Also, keep in mind that everyone grieves on their own timeline and in different ways, so avoidance can look different for different people. An avoidant grief style is often an attempt to prevent thinking about a loss, however, avoidant behaviors often result in the opposite effect.[26]

Somatization. Expressing psychological distress in the form of somatic symptoms and seeking medical help for these. People frequently suffer from bodily complaints, like pain, fatigue, perceived cardiac or gastrointestinal issues. This can even be accompanied by, for example, palpitations, dizziness, diarrhea, and limb weakness. For some people, these bodily complaints are not the result of physiological problems, but rather result from psychological issues, like depression or anxiety.[27]

Hyperarousal. A 24-hour state of elevated cognitive and physiological activation, and often associated with insomnia.[28]

Eating Issues. Grief can affect our eating. Sometimes we may eat too much or too little. For example, eating alone (perhaps because of divorce or if a spouse has died) is a risk factor for nutritional vulnerability in later life.[29]

---

26 Schneck et al., 2019

27 Henningsen, 2018

28 Altena et al., 2017

29 Vesnaver, Keller, Sutherland, Maitland, & Locher, 2016

Panic Attacks. Panic is overwhelming fright, fear, or terror, and it can happen to any person and, at times, can even make you feel as though you are having a heart attack or that you are dying.[30] Typically, a panic attack is short-lived and often related to a frightening event. However, if panic occurs unrelated to situations, is frequent, and is followed by at least 30 days of worrying that you may have another panic attack, this can be panic disorder.[31]

---

30 Torpy, Burke, & Golub, 2011
31 Torpy, Burke, & Golub, 2011

EXERCISE: MY GRIEF'S IMPACT

Looking at the list of grief impacts (somatization, avoidance, hyperarousal, eating issues, panic attacks), can you recognize any unhealthy grief impacts affecting you? Are there other ways that grief is impacting you that are not listed? If so, name these too.

How have loss and grief impacted you in the past?

How are loss and grief impacting you now?

Example: Carrie's Grief Impact

After Carrie's boyfriend of many years left her, she turned to food to fill the void. This was nothing new; for Carrie, over-eating had long been her established pattern whenever she experienced relationship struggles. This tendency had resulted in both unhealthy weight gain and an unhealthy relationship with food.

Working with a therapist, Carrie was able to recognize that it was not food she was actually hungry for in these situations—she was hungry for *connection*. Carrie eventually learned to reach out to friends and family to feed her need to feel close to others, and she was able to minimize her tendency to self-soothe by overeating.

SYMPTOMS OF GRIEF

Symptoms of grief can be broad and vary from person to person. However, general grief symptoms most often include profound sadness, disbelief, longing, and somatization (physical symptoms).[32] In cases of death, the bereaved person's grief symptoms can also involve seeing or hearing the dead loved one.[33] Initially, these symptoms can overtake us and even consume us, but over time, grief symptoms generally subside.[34] It is normal and, yes, even healthy for feelings of grief to follow loss. However, it is important that we recognize potential grief complications, such as severe grief feelings or prolonged grief feelings, which can require professional support.

---

32 Shear, 2011; Thimm & Holland, 2017

33 Shear, 2011; Thimm & Holland, 2017

34 Thimm & Holland, 2017

EXERCISE: DRAWING MY GRIEF SYMPTOMS

When we experience loss, this can often result in physical symptoms (somatization). Use the stick-figure below to draw where you tend to feel grief in your body. For example, after a loss some people may experience physical symptoms such as gastrointestinal issues, muscle tension, headaches, heart palpitation, teeth grinding, fatigue, etc. How does your body physically feel grief? Identify where in your body you feel symptoms and label each symptom.

Figure 2: Drawing My Grief Symptoms

YEARNING AND SEARCHING

Grief's hallmark emotion is yearning. Yearning can create an intense desire to once again see, hold, and have that which we lost. In loss, our brain can instinctively search (often at a subconscious level) in an attempt to find what we lost, even in cases where our loss was the death of a beloved person or pet. For example, when our family dog died, my brain briefly would mistake our neighbor's barking dog for our dog that passed. Logically, I knew my dog was dead and my rational brain accepted they would not return, yet parts of my brain still seemed to search for our lost pet. Another example of this phenomenon involves thinking we saw a familiar face perhaps in a crowd, even when we did not. A man I knew shared with me how, after moving into a new town, he would catch imagined glimpses of a loved one who had passed away as his brain would ever so briefly mistake the familiar face of the lost loved one for the new unfamiliar faces he encountered in the new town. This man said it was as if his brain was tricking him into seeing the person he missed most.

This phenomenon of our brain's continued searching for what we lost, even when the lost can no longer return to us, can in part be explained through neuroscience's explanation[35] involving the conflict between semantic knowledge and episodic knowledge. The continued mental prevalence of the beloved/desired person or thing's existence within our mind (semantic knowledge) can be in conflict with the reality of that person or thing being forever gone (episodic knowledge). This creates in our brain a "gone-but-also-everlasting" experience.[36] Simply put, the brain's yearning and searching can continue and conflicts with the reality that they are gone.

---

35 O'Connor & Seeley, 2022
36 O'Connor & Seeley, 2022, p.2

EXERCISE: YEARNING AND SEARCHING

In what ways have you found yourself yearning for someone or something lost?

Describe times when you caught yourself searching, even for an instant, for someone or something lost even though you rationally knew the person, pet, or thing was not there or could not be found.

Example: Joel's Yearning

Joel's son had been struggling for many years with an inner conflict that eventually resulted in the son's suicide. For Joel, it felt like his world had shattered. Slowly, Joel began to the process of healing his brokenness and eventually accepted his son's death, but he continued to long to see his son, even just one more time.

Many months after his son's death, Joel's condition had not improved. He would hear his son's voice or glimpse his son's face in a crowd, only to realize it was not him and experience his loss all over again. Joel so dearly yearned to see and hear his son that, even though he knew logically that his son was gone, Joel's brain continued searching for him. In time, Joel was able to connect to his son's memory in healthier ways, enabling Joel to both move forward in his grief while still feeling connected to his son.

EXERCISE: MY PERSONAL GRIEF MODEL

How do you grieve? Do you cry and, if so, do you shed these tears only when alone or do you feel comfortable crying in public? Do you listen to music after a loss and, if so, what type of music? Do you seek comfort from family or friends? Or do you prefer to be alone? These are just some of the ways people grieve. Take time now to examine how you grieve—your current personal grief model. Try not to judge yourself or be tempted to insert ways you wish that you grieved, just be honest and list how you actually grieve at the present time. (Note: in the last chapter of this workbook, you will get to re-create your own improved personal grief model by applying healthy tools and techniques you will learn in this workbook.)

HOW I CURRENTLY GRIEVE	WHO OR WHAT TAUGHT ME TO GRIEVE THIS WAY?	IS THIS HEALTHY OR UNHEALTHY FOR ME?
Ex. I sit in my room alone.	Ex. I learned this from my mom.	Ex. This has often been unhealthy for me. I isolated when I really need the help of others.

 Chapter 2

OVERVIEW OF THE GRACE GRIEF MODEL

Topic: An Introduction to the GRACE Grief Model

Exercises & Tools

- GRACE Grief Map: *World View*
- Examining Core Beliefs
- My Core Beliefs and Assumptions
- Thinking About My Losses
- Naming My Losses
- My Personal Grief Timeline
- Knowing My Grief Levels
- My Grief Progress
- How Are You Doing…Really?
- Mood Tracking
- Self-Care
- Activity Scheduling
- Breath Work
- Progressive Muscle Relaxation

THE GRACE GRIEF MODEL

The GRACE Grief Model is a new grief model I created that supports healthy healing from loss. The GRACE model provides hope for those who have been stalled or stuck in their grief journey. This model highlights a way forward by offering new approaches to work through loss, and by offering an expanded understanding of grief that is biologically imperative, emotionally healing, and spiritually nurturing.

The GRACE Grief Model offers five steps toward healing:

Step 1: G – Grief redefined as **G**ood, **G**oing to ebb and flow, and ultimately a **G**ift

Step 2: R – **R**e-story the loss narrative

Step 3: A – **A**dopt new healthy ways to grieve

Step 4: C – **C**onnect with self and others

Step 5: E – **E**ngage in a new normal within a livable pattern of grief work

The GRACE Grief Model (also referred to in this text as the GRACE model or simply GRACE) affirms healthy grieving and offers a powerful, evidenced-based opportunity to heal and grow through loss recovery and restoration, including constructing meaning from loss as we move forward in the grief process. The GRACE model meets you wherever you are in your grief journey and provides a map towards healing and wholeness. This model offers an integration of cognitive behavioral therapy (CBT) and narrative therapy elements within a framework that supports individual beliefs, goals, and sense of purpose (meaning making). The goal of this approach is to foster effective healing through an evidenced-based approach aimed at treating those struggling with grief, including prolonged grief.

In the GRACE Grief Model, CBT and narrative therapy elements within a meaning-making framework were selected and incorporated for several reasons:

First, the CBT techniques, in general, target the loss-related processes and focus on symptoms of painful intrusive memories and behavioral avoidance.

Second, narrative therapy techniques can help remove the identity of the person struggling from loss as "the problem" and instead identify loss itself as the problem. Narrative therapy also supports the telling and re-telling of the loss story in ways that promote healing.

Third, meaning-making elements support the overall restoration by helping re-establish connection with valued life goals, including one's own spirituality. In this text, meaning making will be explored primarily through the context of spirituality, as spiritualty can impact one's understanding of grief as well as provide coping resources in dealing with loss.[37] The term "spirituality" used in the GRACE Grief Model, as well as for the purpose of this book, follows Rosmarin's[38] understanding that spirituality is any way of relating to that which is sacred or to a greater reality, and views religion as a subset of the spiritual involving culturally bound or institutional ways of relating to the sacred.

HOW THE MODEL CAN HELP: *A GRACE-FUL SOLUTION*

The struggle with grief is two-fold: people struggle not only from losses, but also because they do not know how to engage in healthy grief work to address those losses. Many have simply never been taught to grieve in healthy ways. The GRACE model offers a new way to grieve and progress through loss, helping those stuck in grief to learn and practice healthier adaptive ways to move forward.

The GRACE Grief Model offers a solution of hope and healing by:

- Promoting loss recovery and restoration

- Encouraging healthy grieving processes

- Supporting a person's unique grief journey and individuality

- Encouraging inclusion of meaning making, including one's personal spirituality, in the grieving process

TOOLS & TECHNIQUES

The GRACE Grief Model offers tools and techniques listed in the following tables, which are commonly used in cognitive behavioral therapy (CBT), narrative therapy, and within the meaning-making model (MMM). The tables identify core components, list the components' primary tools and techniques, and cite the significant psychological impact that the tools and techniques aim to address.

Most, but not all, of the tools and techniques listed in the three tables will be used in this book (those not used include CBT's in vivo exposure and interoceptive exposure, and MMM's assessments). To optimize care, it is recommended that you go through these tools and techniques (as well as ones not listed) guided by a mental healthcare professional.

---

37 Wortmann & Park, 2008

38 2018

Table 1: Components of Cognitive Behavioral Therapy (CBT) for Addressing Grief[39]

Components of CBT	Tools & Techniques	Impact
Cognitive restructuring	Cognitive distortion identification Socratic questioning Problem solving Mindfulness	Anxiety Panic Depression Avoidance Cognitive distortion Eating disorder Stress Hyperarousal Guilt Intrusive thoughts Rumination Catastrophic thoughts
Exposure	*In vivo Imaginal *Interoceptive	Anxiety Avoidance Stress Hyperarousal Separation sorrow
Psychoeducation	Thought journal Mood charting	Anxiety Avoidance Cognitive distortions Eating disorder Guilt Rumination

---

39   Alvarez, Puliafico, Leonte, & Albano, 2019; Boyes, 2013; Kaczkurkin & Foa, 2015

Components of CBT	Tools & Techniques	Impact
Somatic management skills	Breathing Progressive muscle relaxation Goal setting Behavior activation Mindfulness	Anxiety Depression Hyperarousal
Relapse prevention	Check-ins Goal setting Agenda setting Problem solving	Anxiety Panic Depression Avoidance Cognitive distortion Eating disorders Stress Separation sorrow Catastrophic thoughts

These tools/techniques (in vivo and interoceptive) are not used in this book. However, they could be explored with a mental healthcare professional in the therapy setting.

Table 2: Components of Narrative Therapy (NT) for Addressing Grief[40]

Components of NT	Tools & Techniques	Impact
Deconstruction of problem-saturated stories	Externalizing conversations Questioning Visualization	Anxiety Panic Depression Avoidance Cognitive distortion Eating disorder Stress Hyperarousal Guilt Intrusive thoughts Rumination Catastrophic thoughts
Separating the person from the problem	Externalizing conversations Reflection practices	Anxiety Panic Depression Avoidance Cognitive distortion Eating disorder Stress Hyperarousal Guilt Intrusive thoughts Rumination Catastrophic thoughts

---

40　Thompson & Neimeyer, 2014; White & Epston, 1990; White, 2007; Williams-Reade, Freitas, & Lawson, 2014

Components of NT	Tools & Techniques	Impact
Mapping the effects of the problem (explores how the problem impacts life)	Identifying and evaluating effects Trace influence of problem Unique outcomes Outside witness practices (invite outside person to listen and reflect on story) Accountability (emphasis on personal responsibility)	Separation sorrow
Re-authoring our story to create an empowered preferred narrative that offers unique outcomes and produces supportive networks	Thickening (enriching) the story Create alternate stories Accountability (emphasis on personal responsibility) Taking-it-back practice (take back your narrative) Written artifacts (e.g., letters, journals, collages, etc.)	Anxiety Panic Depression Avoidance Cognitive distortion Eating disorder Stress Hyperarousal Guilt Intrusive thoughts Rumination Catastrophic thoughts

Table 3: Meaning Making Model (MMM) Components[41]

Components of MMM	Tools & Techniques	Impact
Minimize discrepancies between global meaning and situational meaning	Questioning Self-appraisals Meaning making skills Integrating spirituality	Spirituality Cognitive distortion Hyperarousal
Spirituality	*Assessments Questioning Integrating spirituality Self-appraisals Meaning making skills	Spirituality
Stress-Related Meaning	Questioning Integrating spirituality Self-appraisals Meaning making skills	Spirituality Cognitive distortion Stress

This tool/technique (assessments) is not used in this book. However, this could be explored with a mental healthcare professional in the therapy setting.

41 Park, Currier, & Slattery, 2017

THE GRACE GRIEF MODEL GRIEF MAP EXPLAINED

The GRACE Grief Model uses the meaning-making framework to create a "map" to guide us forward in the grief process (see GRACE Grief Map on page 26). Again, meaning making centers on beliefs, goals, and sense of purpose, and involves understanding a situation differently and being able to reexamine your beliefs and goals in an effort to reach consistency among them.[42] To begin, it is important to state that, although the map demonstrates linear movement, we must keep in mind that the grief process is not necessarily linear. Everyone's grief is personal and may progress (or digress) in different ways and at different times.

Looking at the GRACE Grief Map, we find that when our beliefs, goals, and sense of purpose (World View) do not align with the meanings we have given to a specific loss (Loss View), this can create an unhealthy meaning of the loss, derailing our healthy grieving process. When this occurs, there are steps forward through which we can move to support our journey from "unhealthy" meaning making to "healthy" meaning making. The steps forward include these actions:

- **Pausing, Stopping, and Reflecting.** Taking time to orient yourself as to where you are regarding your grief (e.g., how you are doing, what you are doing, how you feel, etc.) can provide you essential time and evaluative information that can then support healthy forward progress through your grief journey.

- **Search & Construct** a sense of meaning (in addition to meaning, this can include mattering or significance, purpose, coherence, and reflectivity) that supports healthy beliefs, goals, and sense of purpose.

The primary purpose of the GRACE Grief Map is to bring awareness of how our perceptions and views impact healthy and unhealthy grief processes, as well as offer a stepwise process for moving forward towards healing and wholeness after loss, creating healthy meaning (alignment).

You have already begun working on two of the corresponding GRACE Grief Map elements (World View and Loss View) in the prior chapter's initial exercises. In upcoming chapters, you will work on these two again, as well as the other four elements of the Grief Map.

---

42 Park & Edmonson, 2011

GRACE Grief Model: Grief Map*

Each exercise in this workbook includes elements of the GRACE Grief Map, while the Graphics Key (below) will highlight for you the corresponding area of focus and help you to identify progression along your Grief Map journey.

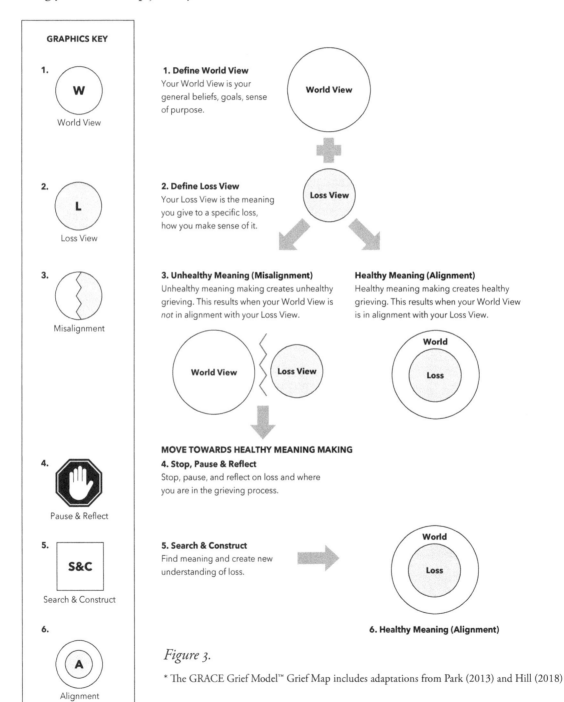

GRAPHICS KEY

1.
W
World View

2.
L
Loss View

3.
Misalignment

4.
Pause & Reflect

5.
S&C
Search & Construct

6.
A
Alignment

1. Define World View
Your World View is your general beliefs, goals, sense of purpose.

World View

2. Define Loss View
Your Loss View is the meaning you give to a specific loss, how you make sense of it.

Loss View

3. Unhealthy Meaning (Misalignment)
Unhealthy meaning making creates unhealthy grieving. This results when your World View is *not* in alignment with your Loss View.

World View   Loss View

Healthy Meaning (Alignment)
Healthy meaning making creates healthy grieving. This results when your World View is in alignment with your Loss View.

World
Loss

MOVE TOWARDS HEALTHY MEANING MAKING

4. Stop, Pause & Reflect
Stop, pause, and reflect on loss and where you are in the grieving process.

5. Search & Construct
Find meaning and create new understanding of loss.

World
Loss

6. Healthy Meaning (Alignment)

Figure 3.

* The GRACE Grief Model™ Grief Map includes adaptations from Park (2013) and Hill (2018)

GRACE GRIEF MAP EXERCISE

Focus #1: Define *World View*

Over the course of reading this workbook, you will examine each of the six components of the GRACE Grief Map:

1. World View
2. View of Loss
3. Healthy and Unhealthy Meanings Constructed about Loss Event
4. Stop, Pause, Reflect
5. Search & Construct
6. New Healthy Meanings Made from Loss

Begin by familiarizing yourself with the GRACE Grief Map. Start with #1. *Define World View* (your beliefs, goals, sense of purpose) by responding to the following questions:

Do you have a broad sense of your World View?

If so, what does this currently include?

What are your general beliefs, goals, sense of purpose in the world?

Is your current World View healthy or unhealthy? Explain your response.

Example: Tricia's Unhealthy World View

Tricia's overall World View was healthy. However, there was one belief that continued to inhibit her ability to move forward.

Tricia grew up with an abusive father and, in time, developed the belief that "all men are bad." As an adult, her general distrust of men resulted in a series of failed personal relationships and even extended into workplace difficulties. Tricia entered professional counseling and with hard work was able to re-examine and challenge this belief. Eventually, she modified her belief and affirmed that not all men are bad. During this time, she was also able to work through lingering past trauma caused by her abusive father.

For Tricia, holding the belief that "all men are bad" was unhealthy, as it disabled her from potential healthy engagement in relationships and kept her stuck in her past. In this way, Tricia's trauma-shaped belief adversely impacted her goals and sense of purpose.

EXERCISE: EXAMINING CORE BELIEFS

W

To help better understand your personal World View (your belief, goals, sense of purpose), begin by listing some of your main core beliefs about the world and about yourself. To help you think about some of your core beliefs, here are a few questions to consider:

Do you believe people are inherently good or bad? Explain your belief.

Do you believe life has to be fair? Why?

Do you believe life has meaning and purpose? Explain your belief.

Do people have souls? What makes you believe this?

What do you believe happens to someone after they die?

What other core beliefs do you hold that you would like to examine? For example, are you struggling with any of your core beliefs? Are you ready to re-examine those beliefs?

CORE BELIEFS

Core beliefs are strong, rigidly held internal beliefs that we hold consistently. Our core beliefs shape how we view ourselves, others, and the world, and can be healthy (adaptive) or unhealthy (maladaptive). It is important to recognize some core beliefs are not accurate and are dysfunctional. Dysfunctional core beliefs are viewed as "persistent attributions that are global, negative and personal regarding life events that are potential risk factors for the recurrence of most psychiatric disorders."[43] Our core beliefs are typically developed early in childhood and continue in one's life, often without challenge or question, and can occur automatically (automatic thoughts). The process of challenging and questioning core beliefs and, subsequently, modifying them as warranted to promote accurate and healthier beliefs, can be highly impactful in supporting one's constructive perceptions.[44]

Challenging Core Beliefs

Beliefs are our understandings formed from a set of assumptions. These assumptions may or may not be true, which then could mean that the core belief, since it's constructed on these assumptions, may or may not be true. Assumptions, whether true or false, are the building blocks from which we construct a belief. It is necessary at times to examine and re-examine our assumptions and determine if they are true or false. True and correct assumptions can reinforce a healthy belief, while false or faulty assumptions can dismantle a healthy belief. Also, it is worthwhile to note that beliefs can be about anything.

On the following page is an example of a core belief followed by an exercise on core beliefs and assumptions. For this exercise, it may be helpful to select one of the core beliefs you expressed in the previous exercise. Write down that core belief and then list the assumptions you hold which created that core belief. Afterwards, review the assumptions individually and challenge them. Are each of your assumptions accurate? Are the assumptions true? Do any of your assumptions perhaps need to be replaced? Does challenging your assumptions lead to any changes in your core belief?

---

43 Delavechia et al., 2016, p. 31
44 Delavechia et al., 2016

Example of Core Belief

My Core Belief: I believe people are inherently good.

My Assumptions: (Assumptions are things we believe as true that ultimately lead to creation of core beliefs.)

- God created all people

- God creates good

- I think all people are born good

- All people are created with choice (free will) and can choose to do good/be good or to do bad/be bad

- While I believe all people are born good, I also believe not every person will choose to do good/be good

Note: Core beliefs do not necessarily involve spiritual beliefs, but sometimes can (as demonstrated in this example).

EXERCISE: MY CORE BELIEF AND ASSUMPTIONS

My Core Belief: Write one of your core beliefs here.		

My Assumptions:

What are the assumptions you have that created this belief? In the spaces below, list each of the assumptions that contributed to the building of the core belief you listed. In other words, write down reasons why you believe what you believe.

Regardless of whether they are true or false, assumptions are the building blocks from which we construct a belief. It is necessary at times to examine and re-examine our assumptions and determine if they are true or false. True and correct assumptions can reinforce a healthy belief while false or faulty assumptions can dismantle a healthy belief.

Figure 4: My Core Beliefs

EXAMINING LOSS

What is loss? For some, loss entails a loved one dying. For others, loss involves many other types of life events ranging broadly in level of severity. Examples of losses include suffering from trauma or abuse (sexual, physical, emotional, psychological, etc.), the rupture of a relationship, struggling with health issues (mental or physical), work failures or being fired or laid off, not getting into the school you wanted, family discord, being bullied as a child, youth, or adult, and parents' experiencing "empty nest" as adult children move away. Of course, these are but a few of the types of losses many incur. In this book, you will have an opportunity to explore your many different, personally-experienced losses.

Your losses may be big or small, recent or old, grieved or ungrieved. In this and upcoming chapters, you will be invited to name losses that you would like to work on and given the opportunity to process your losses. Through this work, you will examine your emotions and feelings associated with loss using the information, tools, and techniques offered.

EXERCISE: THINKING ABOUT MY LOSSES

Begin by creating some time and space to think about your losses. During this set-apart time, reflect on these questions:

Of the losses that I have experienced in my life, which ones most come to mind at this time?

What are your first thoughts when recalling the losses?

On a difficulty scale from 1-100 (100 being the most difficult), how much has each loss impacted you? Rate each loss.

Which of these losses have you grieved?

Which of these losses may be ungrieved?

EXERCISE: NAMING MY LOSSES

Naming losses is an important step in supporting awareness so that you can begin to address losses and associated grief. In psychotherapy, there is a general rule: if we can talk about it, we can treat it. Acknowledging our losses—big and small—helps us to accept them. This initial act of naming losses helps move us forwards in our grief process.

List here the losses that presently come to mind (you may choose to name the same losses identified in the previous exercise. Or you may notice different losses rising to your attention at this time).

Example: A Mother and Sons' Loss of Physical Connection

Like so many others throughout the world, my family was personally impacted by loss during the COVID pandemic in 2020. An especially difficult loss for my family came from our inability to visit my mother-in-law, Bettie Sue, who was battling a chronic terminal illness and lived in an eldercare facility. The prevailing COVID safety restrictions at that time prohibited visiting loved ones in eldercare facilities, hospitals, and other places where vulnerable people resided.

Not being able to spend in-person quality time with Bettie Sue hit especially hard for her two sons, Kirk (my husband) and Keller (my brother-in-law). It felt unbearable for both mother and sons to be separated, especially during what would end up being her last year.

Bettie Sue evaded the COVID virus, but she and her family still suffered from one of its secondary effects—separation from loved ones. For Kirk and Keller, moving forward would require both naming and working through this loss of physical connection.

GRIEF TIMELINE

Grieving itself is an individual process. While grief can impact us collectively and be processed collectively to some extent, each person will react to loss and their emotions around loss in different ways and along their own body's timeline. Many have been raised believing grief must be dealt with quickly, often a result of cultural minimization of the grieving process as many feel uncomfortable dealing with loss. However, your grief journey is just that—yours. You may experience the same loss as someone else and your emotions and reactions may even parallel others, however, your actual grieving process will be as unique as you are. The GRACE Grief Model affirms this individualization of the grieving process and will help you understand and work through your losses in a way that supports your unique needs and maps your unique grief plan.

In order to understand our grief, we must start by gaining awareness of the losses that are impacting us. Using the list you created in prior exercises, create a personal timeline for some of your losses. You may want to begin by focusing on the losses—big or small—that have been the most significant to you. From mourning the loss of a loved one, to experiencing the death of a pet, losing a job, or even having an adult child marry and move away, what makes a loss significant is uniquely specific to you. A loss is anything that feels like a loss *to you*.

EXERCISE:
MY PERSONAL GRIEF TIMELINE

In the space below, create your personal grief timeline using the example as your guide.

Figure 5: Example of Personal Grief Timeline

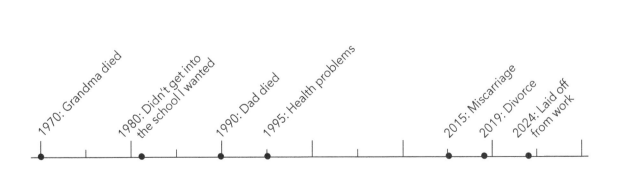

DIFFERENT LEVELS OF GRIEF

We experience grief on different levels and each of these levels involve association with different timeframes—past, present, future. We grieve "what is," which are loss events that are currently occurring (present). We also grieve "what was," which are loss events that have already occurred (past). Additionally, we also grieve the loss of things that *never actually happened,* but that we wish occurred. These losses that never actually happened or never will happen are the loss of what "should have been" (past), the loss of what "should be" (present), and the loss of what "could be" (what could have been) (future).

For example, if a person's grandfather died years ago, that person may be grieving the death of the grandfather as an actual event that happened ("what is" or "what was"), but this person could also be grieving those things that never actually happened or will never happen because their grandfather passed.

- **"What Is"** (e.g., grandpa is dying or grandpa is dead). This is grief about a loss **Currently Occurring** in the **Present.**

- **"What Was"** (e.g., grieving that grandpa died). This is grief about a loss that **Actually Occurred** in the **Past.**

- **"What Should Have Been"** (e.g., sad because they never reconciled after a fight with grandpa). This is grief about something that **Never Occurred** in the **Past.**

- **"What Should Be"** (e.g., upset they cannot call their grandpa today and speak with him, see him, or hug him). This is grief about something that **Will Not Occur** in the **Present.**

- **"What Could Be"** (e.g., grieving that they will never be able to spend another holiday with their grandpa or go fishing again with him). This is grief about something that could have been but **Will Never Occur in** the **Future.**

EXERCISE: KNOWING MY GRIEF LEVELS

Using the Grief Timeline example provided earlier, see below how different levels of loss might look for this person. Note: in the example below, the past, present tense (today), and the future have been added.

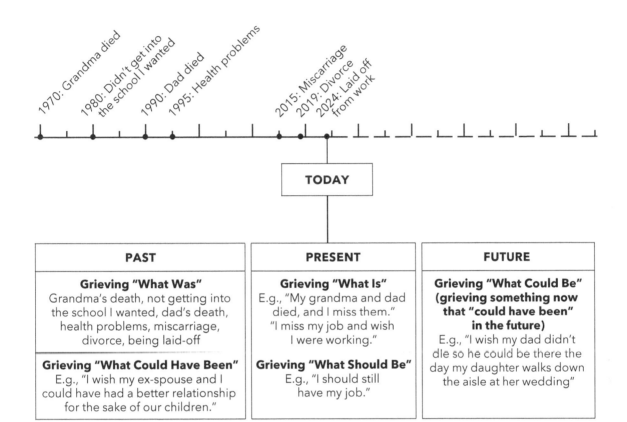

PAST	PRESENT	FUTURE
Grieving "What Was" Grandma's death, not getting into the school I wanted, dad's death, health problems, miscarriage, divorce, being laid-off	**Grieving "What Is"** E.g., "My grandma and dad died, and I miss them." "I miss my job and wish I were working."	**Grieving "What Could Be" (grieving something now that "could have been" in the future)** E.g., "I wish my dad didn't die so he could be there the day my daughter walks down the aisle at her wedding"
Grieving "What Could Have Been" E.g., "I wish my ex-spouse and I could have had a better relationship for the sake of our children."	**Grieving "What Should Be"** E.g., "I should still have my job."	

EXERCISE:
KNOWING MY GRIEF LEVELS

Review your personal grief timeline (page 37) and then consider the different levels of grief shown below. Next, revise your personal grief timeline to include your grief level for each of the losses that you listed. Notice how the five grief levels each correspond to past, present, and future. So, for example, a young girl whose father died may already be grieving that her dad will not be there in the future to walk her down the aisle at her wedding. She is grieving "what could be," which is grieving in the present about something in the future.

Grief Levels:

1. **"What Was"**—grief about a loss that actually occurred in the PAST

2. **"What Should Have Been"**—grief about something that never occurred in the PAST

3. **"What Is"**—grief about a loss that is currently happening in the PRESENT

4. **"What Should Be"**—grief about something that will not occur the PRESENT

5. **"What Could Be"**—grief about something that will never occur the FUTURE

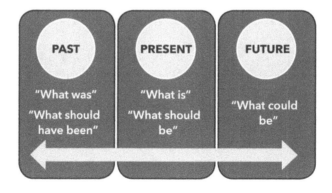

Figure 6: Grief Levels Timeline

MY CURRENT GRIEF PLAN

For a healthy grief journey, we need healthy tools and techniques to support our healing process. One tool to help you recover and move forward from loss is a grief plan, but before you can create a new healthy grief plan you must first take a look at your existing grief plan. To begin, complete the questions below by filling in as much information and detail as you can.

My primary losses are:

Ways these losses are impacting me include:

My current plan for dealing with these losses include:

EXERCISE: MY GRIEF PROGRESS

The task of grief can be work, and this work may seem overwhelming at times. Listing your personal intentions can keep you better focused and help manage your progress. What have been your personal plans regarding your grieving process?

How has your current grief plan been working for you so far? In what ways might your current grief plan be lacking?

How might your World View (beliefs, goals, sense of purpose) and Loss View (meaning you give to a specific loss, how you make sense of that loss) be informing or impacting your grief plan?

How has your current grief plan been healthy or unhealthy for you?

EXERCISE: HOW YOU ARE DOING…REALLY?

You may just now be realizing the plan you currently have for dealing with your grief is not working. You may also recognize some of your current ways of coping with loss (your tools) are either not helping or may even be unhealthy or harmful. As you move forward through this workbook, you will learn new tools to create a healthy grief plan for dealing with loss in healthy ways.

Are you currently progressing in your grief at a pace that feels right for you? Or do you feel like you may be grieving either too fast or too slow? Has your grieving process ever stalled and have you ever become stuck in grief? Think about these questions and share your responses with a trusted person, such as a family member, friend, or your mental health professional.

Name the person with whom you want to discuss your grief progress and the pace of your grieving. Now, take a minute to consider if this is the best person with whom to have this conversation. Is there another person more apporpriate or better qualified to speak with about this? If so, who might this alternate person be? When do you plan to have this discussion? Outline the conversation you plan to have. What are the main topics you want to share? Are there any matters you either do not want to share or feel you may not yet be ready to share?

EXERCISE: MOOD TRACKING

How do you feel today? How did you feel yesterday? Tracking your moods can provide useful insight along your road to recovery after a loss. Begin here by logging your mood/s each day. Try doing this daily for a week, a month, or maybe even longer.

Day	Mood	Scale of 1-10	Comments
Ex.: Monday	A.M. Sad	7	Woke up upset about losing my job.
	MID-DAY Sad	3	Felt better after starting my day and after visiting with job recruiter.
	P.M. Hopeful	6	Have renewed hope that I can find a new job.
Day 1	A.M.		
	MID-DAY		
	P.M.		
Day 2	A.M.		
	MID-DAY		
	P.M.		
Day 3	A.M.		
	MID-DAY		
	P.M.		

Figure 7. Daily Mood Chart

EXERCISE: SELF-CARE

Self-care goal-setting is one way to support the grieving process. Sometimes, after a loss, even basic self care (e.g., bathing, brushing your teeth, proper grooming, getting enough rest, exercise, etc.) can feel difficult. What are your current self-care goals? What changes need to be made at this time to better support a healthier self-care routine for you? How is grief impacting your self-care?

SMART Method

If we set goals, we are more likely to reach them. When setting your goals, try using the S.M.A.R.T.[45] method to make sure your goals are *specific (S), measurable (M), achievable (A), realistic (R)*, and *time-based (T)*. Often times, people who are grieving find it difficult to set goals, but doing so can help bring back a sense of normalcy and help you move forward. Using the S.M.A.R.T. method, write your new goals for self care. Use the table below to begin. Write at least five goals to encourage you to take better care of yourself. Check to see if your goals follow the S.M.A.R.T. method. An example is provided.

My Self-Care Goals	Specific	Measurable	Achievable	Realistic	Time-based
Ex. Eat breakfast every morning this week	☑	☑	☑	☑	☑

Figure 8: Self-Care Goals

---

45 Doran, 1981

EXERCISE: ACTIVITY SCHEDULING

When you review your goals for the week, can you think of any new activities you may need to add to help better ensure you are taking care of yourself? Examples of activities include things like basic self-care, going for a hike, cooking a new recipe, getting together with family or friends, going to the movies or a museum, listening to music, etc. Come up with at least three possible activites you can add to your week that further support your self-care.

1. _____

2. _____

3. _____

EXERCISE: BREATH WORK

One important technique used to support overall mental health, including the grieving process, is breath work. A primary breathing technique proven useful to address negative emotions and stress is diaphragmatic breathing.[46] Diaphragmatic breathing, also known as deep breathing, is understood as a useful integrative practice utilizing the mind to manage stress and psychosomatic problems.[47] In diaphragmatic breathing, we engage our diaphragm, expanding the belly, and deepen both inhalation and exhalation.

Diaphragmatic Breathing

According to the Cleveland Clinic,[48] the diaphragm, which is the large muscle located at the base of our lungs, is the most efficient muscle used in the breathing process. The process of diaphragmatic breathing results in a decrease in respiration frequency while maximizing blood gases,[49] a process which strengthens the diaphragm, decreases the work of breathing by slowing breathing rate, decreases oxygen demand, and uses less effort and energy to breathe.[50]

Steps for Diaphragmatic Breathing

1. Sit or lie down in a safe and comfortable location, preferably quiet.

2. To help you feel your diaphragm move during breath work, place one hand on your upper chest and your other hand near your diaphragm (just above your belly button).

3. Begin breathing in slowly through your nose and out through your mouth. Do not rush your breath (you don't want to hyperventilate). As you breathe in and out, notice which of your hands is moving more. You should notice the hand by your diaphragm (above your belly button) rising and falling more than your other hand. If your hand on your upper chest is moving more, your breath is staying too much in your upper chest and you are not fully engaging your diaphragm. When you are correctly practicing diaphragmatic breathing, you should notice your belly area rising and falling.

4. You may find it helpful to practice diaphragmatic breathing a couple times a day for up to 5 minutes each time.

---

46 Ma et al., 2017

47 Ma et al., 2017

48 Cleveland Clinic, 2023

49 Ma et al., 2017

50 Cleveland Clinic, 2023

EXERCISE: PROGRESSIVE MUSCLE RELAXATION

Progressive Muscle Relaxation (PMR), originally introduced many decades ago,[51] has been shown to still be potentially very beneficial for grief work.[52] PMR can be done in various ways, and involves relaxing the body's muscle groups.

Today, you will practice Progressive Muscle Relaxation by starting with your toes and progressively working up your body through all the major muscle groups until you reach the top of your head. You will begin by tensing that one muscle group for 10 seconds, followed by relaxing that muscle group for 10 seconds as you release the tension. You will repeat this sequence from your toes to your head.

This alternate tensing and relaxing of muscles can support our awareness of tense muscles allowing for the increased awareness of overall physical sensations. For the average person without physical limitations, Progressive Muscle Relaxation is something you should be able to do a couple times a day if needed.

Steps For Progressive Muscle Relaxation

1. **Sit or lay down** in a safe peaceful area.

2. **Start with relaxing breaths.** Take 3-5 deep cleansing breaths, slowly breathing in and out.

3. **Gently tighten the muscles in your feet** and once tightened, hold that tension for 10 seconds before slowly releasing that muscle group. Afterwards, relax that muscle group for at least 10 seconds before moving to the next set of muscles.

4. **Gently tighten the muscles in your calf area** and once tightened, hold that tension for 10 seconds before slowly releasing that muscle group. Afterwards, relax that muscle group for at least 10 seconds before moving to the next set of muscles.

5. **Gently tighten the muscles in your knees and thighs** and once tightened, hold that tension for 10 seconds before slowly releasing that muscle group. Afterwards, relax that muscle group for at least 10 seconds before moving to the next set of muscles.

---

51 Jacobson, 1938

52 Knowles et al., 2021

> **Pause.** Take a few seconds to scan the prior sets of muscles, paying attention to how they feel. Do they feel strong or weak? Are they relaxed or tight? Did you notice any discomfort? Make a quick mental note of any issues and then re-focus and resume the exercise, moving on to the next muscle group.

6. **Gently tighten the muscles in your pelvic floor area** and once tightened, hold that tension for 10 seconds before slowly releasing that muscle group. Afterwards, relax that muscle group for at least 10 seconds before moving to the next set of muscles.

7. **Gently tighten the muscles in your upper and lower abdominal area** and once tightened, hold that tension for 10 seconds before slowly releasing that muscle group. Afterwards, relax that muscle group for at least 10 seconds before moving to the next set of muscles.

8. **Gently tighten the muscles in your upper chest area** and once tightened, hold that tension for 10 seconds before slowly releasing that muscle group. Afterwards, relax that muscle group for at least 10 seconds before moving to the next set of muscles.

9. **Gently tighten the muscles in your lower back area** and once tightened, hold that tension for 10 seconds before slowly releasing that muscle group. Afterwards, relax that muscle group for at least 10 seconds before moving to the next set of muscles.

10. **Gently tighten the muscles in your upper back area and shoulders** and once tightened, hold that tension for 10 seconds before slowly releasing that muscle group. Afterwards, relax that muscle group for at least 10 seconds before moving to the next set of muscles.

> **Pause.** Take a few seconds to scan the prior sets of muscles, paying attention to how they feel. Do they feel strong or weak? Are they relaxed or tight? Did you notice any discomfort? Make a quick mental note of any issues and then re-focus and resume the exercise, moving on to the next muscle group.

11. **Gently tighten the muscles in your arms and hands** and once tightened, hold that tension for 10 seconds before slowly releasing that muscle group. Afterwards, relax that muscle group for at least 10 seconds before moving to the next set of muscles.

12. **Gently tighten the muscles in your neck and head, including face,** and once tightened, hold that tension for 10 seconds before slowly releasing that muscle group. Afterwards, relax that muscle group for at least 10 seconds before moving to the next set of muscles.

13. **We end with relaxing breaths.** Take 3-5 deep cleansing breaths, slowly breathing in and out. You are now ready to gently rise and go about your day.

Note: If you noticed any concerning *emotional* tension or pain, this is something you should share with your mental healthcare professional. If you noticed any concerning *physical* tension or pain, this is something you should share with your medical doctor.

 Chapter 3

GRIEF REDEFINED

Topic: Learning ways to redefine grief as something good, something which is going to ebb and flow in a cyclical pattern, but which ultimately can be viewed as a gift

Exercises & Tools

- GRACE Grief Map: *Loss View*
- GRACE Grief Map: *World View and Loss View, Alignment or Misalignment*
- Grief is Good
- Grief Ebbs and Flows
- Grief is Ultimately a Gift
- GRACE Grief Model *Grief Wave* and Self Check
- GRACE Grief Model *3 Steps for Processing Feelings*
- Anticipate and Plan for Grief Triggers
- Grief Quilt

A NEW UNDERSTANDING OF GRIEF

The emotions of loss, including pain and suffering, are part of our human condition. Everybody hurts from loss at some time. Buddhists acknowledge this suffering through their teaching of the Four Noble Truths: 1) the truth of suffering; 2) the truth of the cause of suffering; 3) the truth of the end of suffering; and 4) the truth of the path that leads to the end of suffering. Christians also are taught in scripture that pain and sorrow will be part of everyday life (John 16:33; Acts 14:22). There is a process we must travel when moving from pain and suffering into a place of hope and peace. The GRACE Grief Model offers this process. In the GRACE model, grief, including all its sorrow, is understood as a remarkable process inviting opportunities for healing.

What is grief, really? In the GRACE Grief Model, grief is redefined:

- Grief is GOOD,

- Grief is GOING TO EBB & FLOW (it is cyclical), and

- Grief is a GIFT.

When understood as *good, going to ebb and flow (cyclical),* and a *gift,* grief can provide a way of helping you progress through difficult emotions, such as pain and suffering, and move towards healing and a hopeful future story. In the upcoming units, you will learn why grief is indeed good, explore the cyclical nature of grief, learn to anticipate and accept grief's approach, and open yourself to regard grief as a gift to be invited into your life.

GRIEF IS GOOD

Waves of loss ebb and flow throughout our lives, but within these murky waters, hope floats. In each new wave of loss, we find the opportunity to heal. In our sorrow we are presented a chance to feel, to name, and to learn from our wounded places. Among the brokenness, we can find the gift grieving brings—the opening to move from pain to peace, from heartbreak to hope.

The emotions of grief can be extremely difficult, but essential to our growth, restoration, and healing. Grief is, in fact, good. Yet grief certainly does not feel good, so how is grief good? Grief is good because, if we grieve in healthy ways, *grief is how we heal from loss.*

WE ARE HARD-WIRED TO HEAL FROM LOSS

You are wonderfully made. You were formed out of flesh and bones, but you were also formed out of stardust.[53] Every person's body is made up of atoms that are billions of years old.[54] Our bodies are hard-wired with insight and intuition that is formed from your very DNA. Your body has innate wisdom, and that innate wisdom includes mechanisms to help us heal.

When our bodies are injured, they innately attempt to heal themselves, much like the scab that forms to heal a skinned knee or the bones that knit themselves back together following a break. While at times we may need support for our healing processes, the body is still remarkably adept

---

53 Schrijver & Schrijver 2015

54 Schrijver & Schrijver, 2015

at trying to mend itself. This innate healing process includes our body's attempt to recover from losses. Losses are a natural and inevitable part of every life, like a thread that weaves in and out of the fabric of our life's narrative. The body is remarkably created to heal from losses through an innate process, and we call this process grieving.

GRACE GRIEF MAP EXERCISE

Focus #2: Loss View

Where do you see yourself right now regarding your grief journey? Review the grief map on the following page. Describe where you think you are in your personal grieving process. We have previously explored *World View* on the GRACE Grief Model Grief Map. Now, we will focus on the second component of the Grief Map, which is your *Loss View*. What are your thoughts and understanding about losses in general? What are your thoughts and understandings about your specific loss or one of your losses?

I think this about loss in general:

I think this about my specific loss (note: for the purpose of working through the GRACE Grief Map, it may be helpful to focus on one loss at a time):

GRACE Grief Model: Grief Map*

Each exercise in this workbook includes elements of the GRACE Grief Map, while the Graphics Key (below) will highlight for you the corresponding area of focus and help you to identify progression along your Grief Map journey.

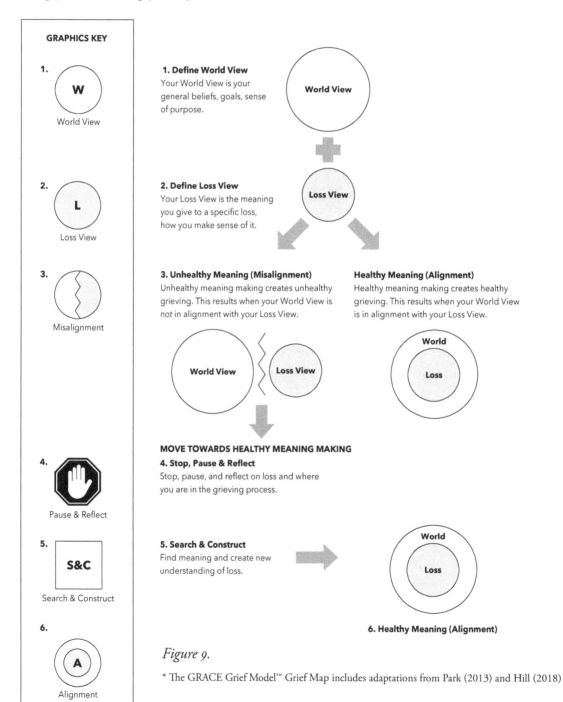

Figure 9.

* The GRACE Grief Model™ Grief Map includes adaptations from Park (2013) and Hill (2018)

GRACE GRIEF MODEL GRIEF MAP EXERCISE

Focus #3: Unhealthy Meanings (Misalignment) vs Healthy Meanings (Alignment)

Where do you see yourself right now regarding your grief journey? Review the GRACE Grief Model Grief Map on the prior page. We have explored World View and Loss View on the GRACE Grief Map. Now, we will focus on the third component of the Grief Map, which is determining if your World View and Loss View are in alignment or misalignment.

In what ways do your World View and Loss View align?

In what ways do your World View and Loss View not align?

Overall, would you say your World View and Loss Views are in alignment or misalignment? Explain here.

Why do you think there may be misalignment between your World View and Loss View?

S&C

EXERCISE: GRIEF IS GOOD

Waves of loss ebb and flow throughout our lives, but within these murky waters, hope floats. In each new wave of loss, we find an opportunity to heal. In our sorrow we are presented a chance to feel, to name, and to learn from our wounded places. Among the brokenness, we can find the gift grieving brings—the opening to move from pain to peace.

The emotions of grief can be extremely difficult, but essential to our growth, restoration, and healing. Grief is, in fact, good, yet it certainly does not feel good. Grief is good because, if we grieve in healthy ways, **grief is how we heal from loss.**

Do you believe grief can be good? Why or why not?

In what ways might grief be good?

GRIEF IS GOING TO EBB & FLOW: GRIEF IS CYCLICAL

Grief comes and goes like a wave, it is cyclical. Physics teaches us that waves are disturbances that travel through space and transfer energy from one place to another. Just as water's energy can be collected and transferred into a process that yields electricity, the collective energy within our emotional grief waves can be harnessed and transferred into our healing plan, our healing process, as we direct the energy embedded in feelings towards healing.

Grief does not occur according to rules or necessarily in stages, rather grief occurs on a continuum. Grief is cyclical, it ebbs and flows back and forth, in a continual wave-like rhythm inviting the healing process. Losses—big and small—are part of our normal human condition and every person will experience some type of loss; the longer we live, the more loss we likely will encounter. The feelings and emotions associated with loss are understood as grief. It is within this beautiful ongoing processing of grief that we are invited into the powerful healing process.

Grief remains a constant part of human life. Our charge, our challenge, is to grow and heal *with* grief, using the energy of grief to propel us forward. Rather than fighting against the waves, we can use the energy the waves produce. How can we allow grief in and harness those waves? To begin, instead of relegating grief to a set of actions on a checklist or phases, we must endure and move through quickly, we recognize instead that grief is the underrated harbinger of healing that begs (at times demands) our attention. Grief is not a single storm that blows into our life, but rather like the weather itself—sometimes calm and sometimes turbulent, but always present. Ocean waves are predominantly created by weather, specifically winds moving across the water's surface. Winds of loss will always move across life's surfaces. As with the weather, grief impacts us continually and is itself necessary for our human existence. The key is to remember this is good and learn to direct and accept its energy as healing properties.

EXERCISE: GRIEF EBBS AND FLOWS

"Grief is cyclical, it ebbs and flows back and forth in a continual rhythm inviting the healing process."

S&C

Considering the above statement, in what ways do you experience the ebbs and flows of grief?

How does grief's rhythm of continually coming-and-going make you feel?

How might you consider these ebbs and flows as patterns of healing?

EXERCISE: GRIEF IS ULTIMATELY A GIFT

Loss can be devastating and cause great pain. The grief response most often does not feel like anything we would voluntarily invite into our life, and it certainly may not feel like a gift. So, why do we call grief a gift? Grief is a gift because it offers us healing and growth. Grieving provides us the mechanism for processing painful emotions and healing wounded feelings while gaining insight that moves us from pain to peace, from hopeless to hopeful.

Our ability to heal and grow comes from moving through grief, which means moving through the feelings and emotions of loss. The GRACE Grief Wave exercise in this unit can help you become aware of how you react to feelings and emotions associated with loss. The GRACE Grief Model's *3 Steps for Processing Feelings* technique can provide guidance on how to deal in healthy ways with the often overwhelming feelings and emotions of loss. Using the *3 Steps for Processing Feelings,* you will learn to:

1. Feel your feelings (supports self-awareness)

2. Name your feelings (validates)

3. Learn and grow from your feelings (process and heal)

These steps can promote adaptive healing from losses big and small.

In what ways does grief *not* feel like a gift?

In what ways might you consider grieving as a gift?

GRACE Grief Model: Grief Wave

Let us review the Grief Wave. As we discussed earlier, the Grief Wave illustrates how the feelings and emotions of loss move in and through our lives. Grief emotions are similar to waves rolling in and out of our lives, and at times these waves can roll over us, tumbling us to the ground. This wave metaphor is also helpful as we learn and practice the GRACE Grief Model 3 Steps for Processing Feelings, a process for helping us learn how to deal with the emotions of loss.

To begin, imagine you are on a seashore. It's a nice calm day.

Now imagine that you begin to feel grief, like a wave of emotion coming towards you.

Too often, rather than experiencing that wave of grief, we BLOCK that

But soon after, a new wave will come—another wave of grief arrives. And again, too often, we will continue blocking these new waves of feelings and emotions. We block our emotions and feelings in many ways, such as self-medicating, over-eating, over-working, etc.

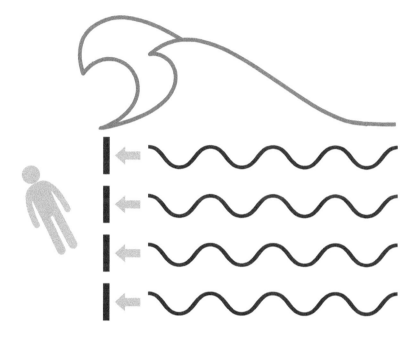

But the pattern continues...until finally the waves of feelings and emotions are simply too much, and they become like a tidal wave that can knock us down.

EXERCISE: SELF-CHECK

How are the waves of grief impacting you now?

What concerns or thoughts do you have about allowing the waves of grief to wash by you and actually allowing yourself to feel your grief feelings, to identify each specific feeling, and to learn from these feelings?

EXERCISE: 3 STEPS FOR PROCESSING FEELINGS

Name a loss you are struggling with now.

STEP 1: FEEL

Support Awareness of Feelings and Healthy Expression of Feelings

Allow yourself some dedicated alone time to feel any feelings you may have associated with that loss. (If you begin to feel too overwhelmed, stop and resume this exercise with your mental healthcare professional.) This is the time to express feelings in healthy ways. Do not judge your feelings, just allow yourself to honestly feel whatever comes. For example, if you are truly sad and feel like crying, allow yourself to feel sad and cry. Try not to judge the feelings as they come, but rather focus on just allowing them and accepting them. (Tip: You'll want to provide space and time for yourself to experience your feelings and emotions.)

STEP 2: NAME

Validate Feelings

Write down each specific feeling you experienced from step 1. Use this list to help you name every feeling you had during this exercise. Remember, do not judge your feelings; just list them.

STEP 3: LEARN & GROW

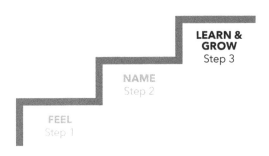

Process and Heal

Now that you have allowed yourself to feel your feelings and named each of those feelings, consider how these feelings and the information we associate with them may help us learn, grow and heal. I believe our bodies are hard-wired to heal whenever possible, including from losses of all types. Just as a skinned knee will scab over or a broken bone will knit itself back together, our bodies were also created to heal from loss, and this is done through the process of adaptive grief work.

What insight can you glean from feeling and sitting with your emotions? What wisdom might you gain from allowing yourself this time and space to actually feel and process each of your emotions associated with this loss? You may find it helpful to answer these questions specific to each different emotion you felt and listed.

Review the GRACE Grief Map (page 54) and consider how you might incorporate the *3 Steps for Processing Feelings* into your grief plan.

EXERCISE: ANTICIPATE AND PLAN FOR GRIEF TRIGGERS

Grief triggers are sudden reminders of a loss. For example, triggers can include driving by the hospital where a loved one died, reading about the company you retired from, or hearing a baby's cry after a pregnancy loss. While triggers are more common earlier in the grief process, triggers can occur at any time. These triggers create emotional waves, which need to be processed. When possible, anticipating and planning for triggers can be very helpful.

Anticipating Grief Triggers

Understanding grief triggers occur and anticipating these triggers is the first step. Below are some common grief triggers. Which ones have triggered your grief?

Photos	Transitions	Smells
Videos	Physical touch	Certain people
Anniversary events	Specific places	TV Shows
Songs	Changes	News stories
Holidays	Movies	Foods

What other grief triggers have you experienced?

When and where do your grief triggers seem to occur?

How are your grief triggers impacting you?

S&C

EXERCISE: GRIEF QUILT

Our many seemingly disparate feelings of grief are actually part of a broader tapestry. These different feelings can come together, much like the pieces of a quilt, to ultimately help us heal. To support your awareness of your own grief feelings, create a drawing in each square of a three-by-four grid to represent each of your feelings regarding a loss. For example, if you feel down you may want to draw a sad face. You are also welcome to use photographs you have taken or cut-out drawings from magazines, etc. to create your grief quilt.

 Chapter 4

RE-STORY YOUR LOSS NARRATIVE

Topic: Re-storying your loss narrative

Exercises & Tools

- The Problems of Grief
- GRACE Grief Map: *Search & Construct*
- My Grief Story
- Imaginal Work
- Removing Our Identity as "The Problem"
- Labels and Grief
- One Who Grieves vs. "The Griever"
- Mapping Effects of "The Problem"
- Catastrophizing
- Re-Writing My Loss Story
- Sharing My Story

WIRED FOR STORIES

Humans are storytellers by design. Stories are how we learn to experience our world, make sense of our world, and share our world. Loss events are no exception. When we experience a loss, our brain attempts to create a story around the loss, including what happened, why it happened, how it happened, and how the loss impacts us. Story telling is central to personal meaning-making and sense-making, as well as communal learning and shared experiences.[55] It is through stories that our brain creates and challenges assumptions, leading to the construction (or de-construction) of beliefs.

Not every story our mind constructs is true. One dilemma is that our mind will attempt to fill in the blanks of a story as it seeks to complete a pattern. In this effort, however, our minds really can play tricks on us. Take the example of loss in which there is often a great amount of stimuli occurring around that loss event—before, during, and after. At times, there is simply too much surrounding the loss for our brains to take in, and so our brains are left with puzzle pieces rather than a complete picture. Here, the brain will attempt to fill in the gaps with assumptions and even created memories. The result is a manufactured storyline that may miss important truths. Another challenge when constructing a story is the temptation to fixate on certain details, as in cases of loss. It is as if our brain selects and hyper-focuses on narrow aspects of the loss story, which then forms a narrow problem-saturated version of the narrative we tell ourselves.

"The Problem"

In addition to supporting a healthier fuller narrative, narrative therapy can be helpful in that it conceptualizes people as separate from the problems. In narrative therapy, problems are viewed as narrow and limiting client stories that do not align with the preferred experiences of self.[56] When I work with people whose loved one died, some therapeutic models (including cognitive behavior therapy) would suggest we identify "the problem" within the person grieving. However, "the problem" lies not necessarily within the griever, but rather "the problem" is that their loved one died. Narrative therapy allows us to recognize and address the real "problem" in these cases.

Goals of Re-Story

Goals of the "re-story" step in the GRACE Grief Model are akin to those of narrative therapy, which include: support the re-authoring of stories through core processes that include the deconstruction of problem-saturated stories, externalization of the story separating the client from the problem, mapping the effects of the problems, and re-authoring and creating a preferred narrative that offers unique outcomes and produces supportive networks for the client.[57] However, the GRACE Grief Model expands on narrative therapy goals in that the GRACE model also attempts to support re-mapping of the grieved brain to support adaptive healthy grieving.

---

55 Peterson, 2017
56 White & Epston, 1990; Williams-Reade, Freitas, & Lawson, 2014
57 White & Epston, 1990; Williams-Reade, Freitas, & Lawson, 2014

GRACE Grief Model: Grief Map*

Each exercise in this workbook includes elements of the GRACE Grief Map, while the Graphics Key (below) will highlight for you the corresponding area of focus and help you to identify progression along your Grief Map journey.

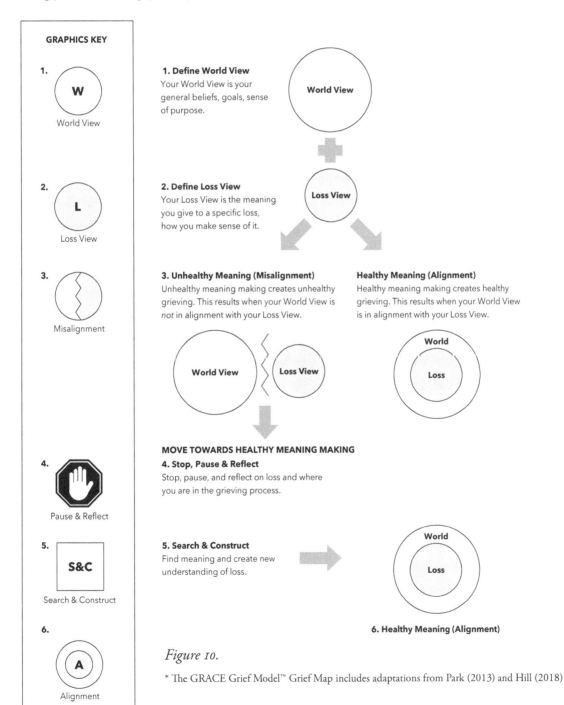

1. Define World View
Your World View is your general beliefs, goals, sense of purpose.

2. Define Loss View
Your Loss View is the meaning you give to a specific loss, how you make sense of it.

3. Unhealthy Meaning (Misalignment)
Unhealthy meaning making creates unhealthy grieving. This results when your World View is *not* in alignment with your Loss View.

Healthy Meaning (Alignment)
Healthy meaning making creates healthy grieving. This results when your World View is in alignment with your Loss View.

MOVE TOWARDS HEALTHY MEANING MAKING
4. Stop, Pause & Reflect
Stop, pause, and reflect on loss and where you are in the grieving process.

5. Search & Construct
Find meaning and create new understanding of loss.

6. Healthy Meaning (Alignment)

GRAPHICS KEY

1. **W** — World View
2. **L** — Loss View
3. Misalignment
4. Pause & Reflect
5. **S&C** — Search & Construct
6. **A** — Alignment

Figure 10.

* The GRACE Grief Model™ Grief Map includes adaptations from Park (2013) and Hill (2018)

EXERCISE: THE PROBLEMS OF GRIEF

What type of problem is grief causing or has grief caused in your life? How could you begin to address this problem in better and healthier ways?

In your grief plan, have you included *stop, pause, and reflect*? If not, might you be avoiding this activity and, if so, why?

If you have already identified a need to *stop, pause, and reflect,* have you been able to identify which activities you may need to engage in or add to your week to help you? For example, do you need to schedule time on your calendar each week for grief work? Do you find certain techniques (e.g., breath work, journaling, imagined exercises, etc.) helpful in your grief work? If so, consider adding these into your daily/weekly routine. Create a goal to modify your current daily and weekly practices by incorporating healthy ways for you to *stop, pause, and reflect* on your grief. Try doing this by making sure each goal listed is S.M.A.R.T. (specific, measurable, achievable, realistic, time-bound).

GRACE GRIEF MAP EXERCISE

Focus #5: Search & Construct

The fifth component in the GRACE Grief Map is Search & Construct (see GRACE Grief Map on page 69). Here, we learn to find meaning and create understanding around the loss. This can begin by using the GRACE Grief Model exercise and tools, such as those detailed in this chapter, GRACE model's Step 2: Re-Story.

As you work on your loss story and are learning how to re-story, consider the following:

- How long have I been telling myself the same loss story?
- What parts of my loss story are especially difficult?
- Are there parts of the story that I may have wrong?
- Is there more to this story that I might need to consider?

WRITING OUR GRIEF STORYLINE

What is your grief story? Let's begin to identify some of our main thoughts, feelings, and behaviors regarding our grief story. Like many people, your actual grief storyline may include multiples losses or multiple loss events. For example, perhaps more than one person in your family or extended family has died, however, for today's activity we will select just one of those deaths to begin writing about. For this exercise, we will focus on writing down our thoughts, feelings, and behaviors related to this primary loss. If your loss event does not include a family death (like in the example), simply begin writing about whatever loss event you want to explore by filling in the blank table on the following page.

GRIEF STORYLINE (EXAMPLE)

My Loss Event	Ex. My dad died
Thoughts	Ex. I miss my dad. Who will help me with all the things my dad used to do for me? I'm worried about how my mom will do without my dad.
Feelings	Ex. Sad, angry, concerned, afraid, mad, confused, tired
Behaviors	Ex. I cry often. I find it hard to engage with others recently in social settings.

EXERCISE: MY GRIEF STORY

My Loss Event	
Thoughts	
Feelings/Emotions	
Behaviors	

Figure 11: My Grief Storyline

EXERCISE: IMAGINAL WORK

Removing Yourself And Your Label As "The Problem"

Find a quiet, safe place where you can sit relaxed with your eyes closed. Using the ideas and insights you gleaned from the prior exercise, you will now lean further into removing yourself and your label as "the problem" in this imagination exercise.

1. **Imagine ways in which you (or others) may perceive yourself as "the problem" in your loss story.** For example, in what ways do you think or feel that your struggles (e.g., depression, anxiety, etc.) resulting from the loss are because of something you did or did not do?

2. **Think about any evidence that you believe suggests you may be "the problem."** For example, do you perceive any of your thoughts, actions, or behaviors caused "the problem?"

3. **Now, challenge that evidence.** Is it true, is it real? Is there any actual truth in the idea that your thoughts, actions, or behaviors caused "the problem?"

4. **Think about evidence that suggests you are *not* "the problem."** This includes considering evidence that points to your thoughts, actions, or behaviors *not* being the root of the problem.

5. **Consider alternate roots of "the problem."** If this problem is not the result of you (your thoughts, actions, behaviors), then what might have actually caused "the problem?"

6. **Now, imagine you are not "the problem."** What, other than you, could be the actual problem(s) in your loss story? What new perspectives do you gain if you no longer identify as "the problem?"

EXERCISE: REMOVING OUR IDENTITY AS "THE PROBLEM"

After Amare's wife died suddenly in a car accident, he developed clinical depression. Amare blamed himself for not driving her to the store as she had requested on the evening of her fatal car accident. After her death, Amare fell into great despair and, eventually, Amare's sense of self began to suffer as he grew to view himself as "the problem" in his grief story. Amare perceived he was the root-cause of not only his wife's death, but also believed he caused his own suffering and depression. Amare began thinking he would never be happy again and found himself isolating from friends and family as he started drinking too much to numb his pain. Amare needed help, including help realizing he was not "the problem" in this story. In Amare's case, his faulty thinking (cognitive distortion), which led him to believe he caused his wife's death, needed to be challenged and replaced with a healthy thinking. For Amare this included understanding and accepting that he did not cause his wife to die, and that the root-cause of his depression was his wife's death, which he had no control over.

Have you ever thought of yourself as "the problem?" If so, in what ways?

How has thinking about yourself as "the problem" hurt you or others?

Now remove yourself as "the problem" and consider what alternatives (other than you) might actually have contributed to or caused "the problem."

EXERCISE: LABELS AND GRIEF

Language and labels used are important but can become problematic and "too easily become the lens through which patients are solely viewed, thereby subjugating the unique and often more empowering versions of a patient's experience with their treatment regimen."[58] Narrative therapy elements allow for the deconstruction of negative and harmful labels.[59] Deconstructing problem-saturated stories is helpful in "uncovering a patient's personal meaning and significance related to the illness or illness-related problem."[60]

What negative or harmful labels have others called you?

What negative or harmful labels have you answered to?

How and when did you first get the label(s)? Did someone give these labels to you? When and why?

Did you give these labels to yourself? If so, when and why?

---

58   Williams-Reade, Freitas, & Lawson, 2014, p. 3

59   White & Epston, 1990; Williams-Reade, Freitas, & Lawson, 2014

60   Williams-Reade, Freitas, & Lawson, 2014, p. 3

EXERCISE: ONE WHO GRIEVES VS. "THE GRIEVER"

The feelings of loss can seem so strong that, at times, we may begin to accept these feelings as facts. However, it is important to acknowledge that feelings are not facts. Feelings of grief are incredibly important, as they bring opportunities to help us learn, grow, and heal. But at times, we can misunderstand our own feelings about loss.

A common misunderstanding is when people assume the identity of "the griever." Please understand, it is good to grieve. Grief is a normal part of everyone's life, and grief is healthy and necessary. However, remember that grief does not define us; grieving is a process, not who or what we are. The grief feelings can be so powerful at times that we can take on grief, almost like an identity. This is not a healthy identity. We instead want to separate ourselves by understanding we are a person who has grief, we do not want to assume the identity of grief ("the griever"). By not allowing grief to become your identity you can better enable yourself to view grief from a healthier perspective, allowing you to view grief more objectively. Grieving is a process to go through, not an identity to become.

Have you ever found yourself being defined by grief and identified as "the griever?"

If so, how did others respond to you when you behaved as "the griever?" Recall how that made you feel.

How did you feel about yourself in the role of "the griever?"

Visualize yourself as you wish you felt, thought, and behaved (acted) regarding grief.

S&C

A

EXERCISE: MAPPING EFFECTS OF "THE PROBLEM"

Mapping the effects of the problem is another component used in the GRACE Grief Model. Mapping the effects involves identifying and evaluating effects and influences of the problem(s),[61] and after the problem has been identified, in-depth conversations trace the influence of the problem through aspects of a person's life.[62] Mapping enables the exploration of the problem's impact, allowing for an evaluation of the problems' effect.[63]

How is "The Problem" Impacting Your Life?

Think of one of your loss events and explore how the problems associated with this loss have impacted you. Begin to identify and evaluate the effects of this loss in your life by describing how this loss has impacted these major areas of your life:

Name Your Loss:_____

How is loss impacting you in these areas?

- Home life

- Work/school

- Relationships

- Health (physical and mental)

- Spirituality/meaning-making

- Identity

- Future plans

---

61 White, 2007

62 Williams-Reade, Freitas, & Lawson, 2014

63 Williams-Reade, Freitas, & Lawson, 2014

S&C

A

EXERCISE: CATASTROPHIZING

As we tell our stories, sometimes these stories become problem-saturated. At times, the problems within our narrative result from catastrophic thinking. Catastrophizing, which is expecting the worst or only remembering the worst, is irrational and unhealthy thinking and is a type of cognitive distortion (faulty thinking pattern). If you struggle with catastrophic thinking, try this simple exercise to help shift overly negative and unhealthy thoughts to healthier and more realistic ways of thinking.

Name something you catastrophize about. *Ex. When I travel by airplane, I think the plane is going to crash and I will die.*

Now write down your responses to the following three questions as it relates to your catastrophic thought:

1. What's the **worst** that can happen? *Ex. The plane could crash and I could die.*

2. What's the **best** that could happen? *Ex. I have a good safe flight and my worries about crashing are reduced or eliminated.*

3. What's **most likely** to happen? *Ex. Airplane travel is among the safest modes of transportation, so I will likely have a safe flight and again prove to myself planes are a safe way to travel. This will make me feel a little better about future air travel.*

Asking and answering these three questions helps push your brain beyond catastrophic thinking into healthier thought processes. Next time you catch yourself jumping to the worst-case scenario, ask and answer for yourself these three questions.

WRITING AND RE-WRITING OUR GRIEF STORIES

As we move through our grief journey, we develop the stories we tell ourselves and others about our loss. Sometimes these stories are healthy and move us forward in our grief process, but sometimes they are unhealthy and keep us stuck in our grief. For many, it is time to examine or re-examine the stories and, when needed, re-write our loss story in fuller and healthier ways. Re-telling our stories in healthy ways does not mean forgetting about what happened or trying to change facts, rather it means adding important details and insights that bring deeper awareness and healing understanding to our story. The practice of re-authoring stories and developing a preferred adaptive narrative is a goal of the GRACE Grief Model. Re-authoring includes thickening or enriching the story to create the new story.[64] One way re-authoring is achieved is through writing, including diary work, journaling, and letter writing.[65]

---

64 White & Epston, 1990, White, 2007

65 Thompson & Neimeyer, 2014

EXERCISE: RE-WRITING MY LOSS STORY

Using what you wrote in the Catastrophizing exercise, consider what changes and additions you can make to your loss storyline to enrich the story with truthful understandings and new events that add depth, information, and different perspectives. Focus on adding more to broaden your story with details. Try enriching your story with information that is both accurate and helpful.

Name and describe your loss event.

Now reconsider how this loss has impacted you in these areas:

- Home life
- Work/school
- Relationships
- Health (physical and mental)

- Spirituality/meaning-making
- Identity
- Future plans

What new details can you add to your loss event in each of these areas of your life?

What new information can you add that is helpful and enriches your story?

What positive aspects can you incorporate into your story that may have been previously omitted? For example, before/during/after your loss event, were there helpers or people who supported you? If so, who helped you and how did they help you?

Compare how your loss event storyline has changed by looking at your answers from the prior exercise ("How is Loss Impacting Your Life") as compared to your answers in this exercise. What major changes do you recognize? Do these changes evoke any new feelings or thoughts?

EXERCISE: SHARING MY STORY

Now that you have written and re-written aspects of at least one loss story, it is time to share that with another person. Sharing can be helpful in the grieving process and also allows the opportunity for someone else to objectively hear and perhaps even correct or question some of the details of the story we are telling ourselves and others about our loss event.

Identify at least one adult with whom you can share your loss story. Make sure this is someone who knows about this loss, will agree to listen to your story, and who can offer healthy perspective and insight into what you are sharing.

Follow these basic steps:

1. Decide which loss story you want to share (you may want to use the story you explored in the prior two exercises).

2. Select a trusted adult who is familiar with your loss story to share (or re-share) your loss with.

3. Agree on a day and time to meet (in person or video conference is best).

4. During the agreed meeting, share with them your loss story. Then, allow them to share with you their own unique understanding of the same loss event as they heard it told or, perhaps, as they themselves saw or experienced it (please know their story will likely include different perspective and details from yours).

5. Discuss with each other the different perspectives and variations in insights and understanding between how you and they understand and view the loss event.

6. After the meeting, journal the responses and any new understanding or new feelings and thoughts you gained through this exercise.

 Chapter 5

ADOPT NEW HEALTHY WAYS OF GRIEVING

Topic: Incorporating new healthy grief practices into your life, including practices from other cultures and also the incorporation of spirituality

Exercises & Tools

- GRACE Grief Map: *New Healthy Meanings*
- Core Beliefs About Grief and Culture
- Challenging Cultural Core Beliefs
- Describing Grief and Loss With Words (Verbal)
- Expressing Grief and Loss Without Words (Non-Verbal)
- What is Your Spiritual Framework?
- Core Beliefs About Spirituality
- My Spiritual Traditions on Funerals/Celebration of Life
- My Spiritual Rituals
- What Does a Soul Look Like?
- Write Your Own Devotional
- GRACE Grief Model: *3 Steps for Processing Feelings*
- Light a Candle
- What Feeds Your Soul?

HEALTHY GRIEF: INFLUENCES OF CULTURE & SPIRITUALITY

In the exercises in this chapter, we will consider healthy ways to grieve through an examination of both culture and spirituality. We will explore the possibility of incorporating into our own grief processes some of the valuable adaptive lessons and tools we find throughout various cultures and through a deepening of our personal understanding of the sacred. Adopting new healthy ways of grieving can provide us with much needed tools to borrow and use, propelling us forward in our grief journey.

CULTURAL DIFFERENCES

Grief is a "transcultural phenomenon."[66] The stories we share about our losses are often impacted by cultural norms. The emotions of grief also differ across cultures. Grief, therefore, can be contextualized within what is deemed "acceptable" or "not acceptable" based on cultural values, beliefs, and ethics. Culture impacts grief in subtle and not so subtle ways. Some cultural responses to loss can be limiting and impede the grieving process, such as the Eurocentric/American pattern of avoiding or minimizing grief,[67] while other cultural practices can prove healing. It is these healing practices from cultures near and far that I encourage you to explore and, when warranted, adopt into the rhythms of your own grieving patterns. We have much to share and learn from others. Drawing from different cultures helps connect us to a global wellspring of supportive traditions available for our use and healing as we move through our loss journeys.

Diverse Cultures & Diverse Ways Of Grieving

Grief traditions can vary greatly across cultural traditions. We see evidence of this throughout grief work in every country. Some examples of grief traditions across cultures (including spiritual cultures) include New Zealand's Māori tribal Haka dance often performed at funerals; Mexico's *Dia De Los Muertos* celebratory holiday of remembrance for those deceased; the Hindu's sharing of a special meal to memorialize a loved one's passing and affirm their belief in reincarnation; Vietnam's shrines adorned with photos, special items, and candles created in memory of deceased loved ones; and New Orleans' jazz funeral marches that form a parade, led by the casket, taking mourners from the church to the cemetery.

Grief traditions are not the only variation, there also seem to exist cultural variations in how people express grief emotion. Decades ago, Barley,[68] writing on the subject of culture and grief,

---

66 Enez, 2018, p. 277

67 Tyler & Darrow, 2022

68 Barley, 1997

stated that in cases of bereavement Westerners mourn "not a ritual, social or physical state but one of disordered emotions that may require therapy, (while) the dominant emotion at a Chinese funeral may not be grief but scarcely concealed fear of the contagion of death."[69] Religious beliefs influenced by culture also impact grief traditions. "Religious beliefs and practices…are strongly related to culture and may account for some of the variations in grieving processes."[70] For example, as we again examine Chinese tradition, we find influence of fatalism affecting Chinese bereavement as marked by a culture of infrequent sharing of grief emotions. In fact, for the traditional Chinese, the sharing of grief emotion is so atypical, the way many Chinese comfort mourners is by saying "Restrain your grief and accord with inevitable changes."[71]

Individual & Communal Grief Aspects

When discussing emotions, it is important to acknowledge individual and communal aspects. Individually and communally, emotional variance among people may be explained in part due to gender, culture, biology, and environment. Some studies suggest, women show stronger emotional expressiveness whereas men have stronger emotional experiences specific to certain types of emotions, namely anger and positive stimuli.[72] Women are reported to experience more intense emotional responses overall, especially pertaining to negative emotions, whereas men are reported to experience stronger emotional experiences.[73]

According to Nangyeon Lim,[74] emotion, whether viewed as universal or social, is in large part biologically based and also influenced by environment. Some research suggests that the biological basis of emotion involves genetic similarities across cultures, such as facial expressions (e.g., smile when happy, frown when sad) which can be interpreted similarly regardless of culture or geographical location.[75] Culture's impact of emotion is broad and can impact the words and expressions used to describe emotions,[76] as well as how emotions are expressed.[77]

---

69 Barley, 1997, p. 16
70 Stelzer et al., 2020, p. 4
71 Stelzer et al., 2020, p. 4
72 Deng et al., 2016
73 Deng et al., 2016
74 Lim, 2016
75 Lim, 2016; Eckman, 1972
76 Lim, 2016; Shott, 1979
77 Lim, 2016; Heelas, 1986

GRACE GRIEF MAP EXERCISE

Focus #6: New Healthy Meanings

Next, we will explore the sixth component of the GRACE Grief Model Grief Map: new healthy meaning making from loss (see GRACE Grief Map on following page). Progressing to this point on the Grief Map means you have worked to foster a renewed sense of meaning, mattering or significance, purpose, coherence, and reflectivity that reconciles discrepancies between World View and Loss View in adaptive ways that move them forward in their grief journey.

Grief and Culture

Think about how grief is understood and dealt with in your own culture. How are grief feelings and emotions shared or not shared in your culture?

Describe the culture you grew up in.

Describe the culture you live in now, if different.

GRACE Grief Model: Grief Map*

Each exercise in this workbook includes elements of the GRACE Grief Map, while the Graphics Key (below) will highlight for you the corresponding area of focus and help you to identify progression along your Grief Map journey.

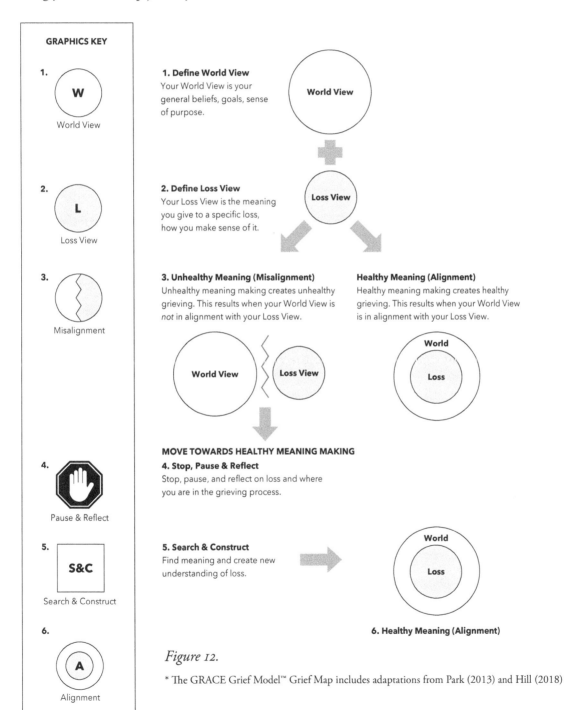

Figure 12.

* The GRACE Grief Model™ Grief Map includes adaptations from Park (2013) and Hill (2018)

EXERCISE: CORE BELIEFS ABOUT GRIEF AND CULTURE

What are your core beliefs regarding loss and grief with regard to the culture you grew up in and, if they differ, the culture you live in now? How has culture impacted how you grieve? In what ways has culture affected how you deal with loss? List some of your core beliefs about loss and grief that have developed because of cultural influences (past or present):

EXERCISE: CHALLENGING CULTURAL CORE BELIEFS

Beliefs are comprised of a set of assumptions. These assumptions may or may not be true, which then could mean the core belief, since it is constructed on these assumptions, may or may not be true. Select one of your core cultural beliefs about grief that you have yet to explore. Write down that core belief and then list the assumptions you hold which created that core belief. Afterwards, review the assumptions individually and challenge them. Are each of your assumptions accurate? Are the assumptions true? Do any of your assumptions perhaps need to be replaced? Does challenging your assumptions lead to any changes in your core belief?

My Cultural Core Belief: Write one of your cultural core beliefs here.		
My Assumptions: What are the assumptions you have that created this belief? In the spaces below, list each of the assumptions that contributed to the building of the core belief you listed. In other words, write down reasons why you believe what you believe.		

Figure 13: Core Beliefs

EXERCISE: DESCRIBING GRIEF AND LOSS WITH WORDS (VERBAL)

Grief is universal and experienced by every person. However, how grief is understood and expressed can vary from culture to culture. Even the words and terminologies we use to describe and talk about loss and grief can be expressed in different ways among different cultures. Consider how culture has informed the words you use and how you talk about loss and grief.

What words come to mind when you think of grief (think about the feelings resulting from the loss event)?

What words come to mind when you think of loss (think of the event that caused the grief)?

Which of these words are emotions?

Do any of the words on your list surprise you?

What are perhaps some new words or expressions you might use to increase a healthy understanding of grief and loss?

EXERCISE: EXPRESSING GRIEF & LOSS WITHOUT WORDS (NON-VERBAL)

Consider how culture has informed the non-verbal ways you express and communicate your grief. In some cultures, certain non-verbal expressions are appropriate, while these same expressions in other cultures are frowned upon or even unacceptable. Non-verbal expressions can include gestures and behaviors, as well as the use of artifacts (objects/things or images) a person may wear or use within their environment.

Some non-verbal grief expressions include:

- Eye contact
- Crying or not crying
- Facial expressions
- Touch (e.g., hug, pat on back, hand-shake, etc.)
- Body movements

- Physical space (proxemics)
- Body posture
- Artifacts (e.g., jewelry or other accessories, photographs, etc.)
- Appearance (e.g., dress)
- Religious or faith-based clothing, symbols, etc.

What non-verbal ways do you currently use to express loss and grief? The list above can serve as a guide, but please also write down any additional expressions not listed that you may also use. Which non-verbal expressions do you find especially healthy for you?

Are there any that are unhealthy for you? If so, which ones?

If any are unhealthy, what might you do to stop these and possibly replace them with other non-verbal expressions that are healthy for you?

S&C

A

EXERCISE: WHAT IS YOUR SPIRITUAL FRAMEWORK?

Spirituality is any way of relating to that which is sacred or to a greater reality.[78] Spiritual matters, including matters of faith, religion, and belief, encompass numerous dimensions,[79] and impact understandings of loss.[80] Spiritualty can impact one's understanding of grief as well as provide coping resources in dealing with loss.[81]

One way that spirituality helps involves bereavement. Our brain maps attempt to link us to lost loved ones within the three dimensions of a relationship: space, time, and closeness.[82] In cases of death, our brain still desires to locate the loved one in a specific place and time, begging the question, "Where are they?" Spirituality can help create an understanding of where our deceased loved one now exists in space and time, and this can facilitate the re-mapping of the brain in healthy ways supporting the grieving process. For example, spirituality may better enable a person to re-orient their relationship to a deceased person, which may place the deceased as now existing in eternity (time) and in realm understood as heaven (place). Or spirituality, for others, may allow an understanding that the deceased exists for now (time) scattered in the universe as stardust (place).

- How do you define spirituality?

- In what ways might you consider yourself spiritual?

- In what ways do you struggle with your spirituality?

- How might your understanding of spirituality be useful to you and incorporated into your grief work?

78 Rosmarin, 2018

79 Wortmann & Park, 2008

80 Park & Halifax, 2011

81 Park, 2013; Wortmann & Park, 2008

82 Huberman, 2022

EXERCISE: CORE BELIEFS ABOUT SPIRITUALITY

What are your core beliefs regarding loss and grief with regard to spirituality? Has spirituality impacted how you grieve? If so, how? What are specific ways spirituality has affected how you deal with loss? List some of your core beliefs about loss and grief that have developed because of your spirituality or lack of spirituality:

S&C

A

EXERCISE: MY SPIRITUAL TRADITIONS ON FUNERALS/CELEBRATIONS OF LIFE

Describe how your spiritual or faith-based traditions have influenced how you deal with loss, including in cases of death.

What funeral or celebration of life traditions do you currently practice after a death in your family, community, or culture?

In your opinion, what should change about the way funerals/celebrations of life and bereavement customs are handled?

Are there any changes you might consider making to the existing funeral/celebration of life and bereavement customs of your family, community, or culture?

EXERCISE: SPIRITUAL RITUALS

Spiritual rituals are those activities we do with regularity that move us into the sacred. They are symbolic rhythms we choose to incorporate into the patterns of our lives. These rituals can be corporate or done in community (such as community worship) or personal and practiced alone (such as private prayer). Additional examples of spiritual rituals that can be either corporate or personal include worship, prayer, singing, music, breath work, nature walks, spiritual journaling, lighting candles, anointing with oil, shared sacred meals, dance, art, etc.

What spiritual rituals do you currently incorporate into your grief work?

Which do you practice with others? Which do you practice alone?

Which new spiritual rituals might you want to consider adding?

EXERCISE: WHAT DOES A SOUL LOOK LIKE?

Many believe in the concept of a soul, the spiritual essence of a person that continues even after death. For those who believe in souls, you are invited now to consider and explore this idea deeper. Use the space below to draw what you believe a soul might look like.

In addition to your drawing (or perhaps in lieu of), write the words that you believe describe a soul's attributes or characteristics.

EXERCISE: WRITE YOUR OWN DEVOTIONAL

What is sacred to you? Who is sacred to you? Honoring the spiritual within ourselves, as well as how we practice our spirituality, is an important part of living into the fullness of who we are, and also important in supporting our healing process through grief. One way to connect to your spirituality is through the use of devotionals. A devotional is a short spiritual or religious writing or service. The purpose of a devotional is to support your spiritual beliefs by creating space and intention for your focus on your Higher Power, the Divine.

In this exercise, you will write a devotional. There is no right or wrong way to write a devotional, so do not be intimidated if you have never attempted this. You may choose to do this exercise in any way you wish. A guideline has been outlined below for you to follow if you prefer.

Start by selecting a short piece of sacred text or any piece of writing that you find spiritual that inspires you (e.g., poem). Write (or attach) your selected text here:

Read and re-read that piece of text. You may also find it helpful to research into the text (e.g., words, context, history, etc.) to further explore and seek to understand what the text says. After a thorough reading and exploration of the text, begin to write down what this text says by considering the following.

1) What do you imagine the author of this text is trying to say to the audience to whom the text was originally written? Consider the historical context.

2) How does this text fit into the author's larger work/s? For example, if your selected text is a verse from the Bible, Torah, or other sacred scripture, how does your verse fit into the larger scope of those sacred writings? What does your text have to say about the nature of the Divine? What does your text have to say about what God wants for you and your life?

3) Since you have already considered the historical context of your text, now consider what you believe the author is trying to convey to you today through this text.

4) What could the author be suggesting you do after having read this text? Consider, for example, if this text is intended to inform you, inspire you, create change within you, and/or compel you to some action.

EXERCISE: GRACE GRIEF MODEL: 3 STEPS FOR PROCESSING FEELINGS

Name a loss you are struggling with pertaining to **spirituality**. (If needed, please work with your mental healthcare professional on this exercise.)

STEP 1: FEEL

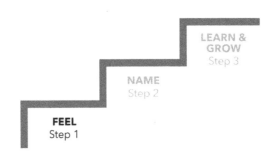

Support Awareness Of Feelings and Healthy Expression of Feelings

Allow yourself some dedicated alone time to feel any feelings you may have associated with that loss. (If you begin to feel too overwhelmed, stop and resume this exercise with your mental healthcare professional.) This is the time to express feelings, and to do so in healthy ways. Do not judge your feelings, just allow yourself to honestly feel whatever comes. For example, if you are truly sad and feel like crying, allow yourself to feel sad and cry. (Allow space and time for yourself to experience your feelings and emotions.)

STEP 2: NAME

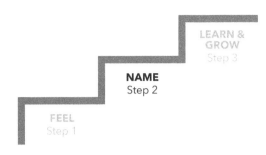

Validate Feelings

Write down each specific feeling you experienced from step 1. Remember, do not judge your feelings; just list them.

STEP 3: LEARN & GROW

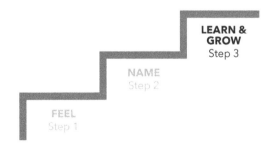

Process And Heal

Now that you have allowed yourself to feel your feelings and named each of those feelings, consider how these feelings and the information we associate with them may help us learn, grow, and heal. You are created of flesh and bones, but you are also created of stardust. You have atoms inside of your body that are billions of years old. There is a lot of innate wisdom in you! I believe our bodies are hard-wired to heal whenever possible, including from losses of all types. Just as a skinned knee will scab over or a broken bone will attempt to knit itself, our bodies were also created through time to heal from loss, and this is done through the process of adaptive grief work.

What insight can you glean from feeling and sitting with your emotions?

What wisdom might you gain from allowing yourself this time and space to actually feel and process each of your emotions associated with this loss? You may find it helpful to answer these questions specific to each different emotion you felt and listed.

Review your Grief Map and consider how you might incorporate the *3 Steps for Processing Feelings* into your plan.

S&C

A

EXERCISE: LIGHT A CANDLE

The practice of lighting a candle for spiritual practices is ancient. The symbolism of the flame and the ritual of lighting the candle have been incorporated into various sacred meanings throughout human history.

Take time now to find a safe place and light a candle. Consider how this simple act might connect you to that which is sacred in your understanding. After lighting the candle, simply sit and observe for approximately 5 minutes. This exercise may be done alone or in the presence of others.

What might this candle or flame represent to you?

As you watch the flame, how do you feel? What thoughts are you having?

What do you regard as sacred or holy in your life? How might this candle help connect you to that which is sacred for you?

After approximately 5 minutes, put out the flame. Now that the candle is extinguished, notice any changes in the feelings or thoughts you may be having.

EXERCISE: WHAT FEEDS YOUR SOUL?

A young man turned to his spiritual leader and confessed, "I feel closer to God when I'm out fishing than when I'm sitting in church." The spiritual leader thought for a moment then replied, "I believe God would rather you be thinking about God as you're fishing than thinking about fishing as you sit in worship. Go enjoy this day out on the water, and I hope to see you again in worship another time soon."

Nourishing our soul, our spirituality, is important and perhaps especially so during the grief journey. For many, connecting to the Divine means connecting to a Higher Power in places that feed their souls. What about you? What feeds your soul? How do you nourish your spirit? Where and when do you feel closest to the Divine or your Higher Power?

 Chapter 6

CONNECT WITH SELF & OTHERS

Topic: Connecting with self and others to promote healthy grieving

Exercises & Tools

- Who Am I?
- Challenge Faulty Thinking
- What Are My Grief Symptoms?
- Turning Down the Grief Volume
- My Loss Storyline
- Journaling to Explore Memories and Emotions
- Behavior Activation: Engaging In Healthy Activities

HARDWIRED FOR CONNECTION WITH SELF AND OTHERS

We are created for connection. Within our individual biology, our atoms link and cells combine. Our bodies are organized to interconnect from within as systems. Externally, we find the very nature of humanity is connection. We seek others for support and survival, and to share our world with. Connecting with ourselves and others supports our grief journey. In this chapter, we will explore connection during times of loss, including connecting with ourselves, connecting with friends and family, and connecting with professional support.

Connecting with oneself can include an examination of who we are in light of loss. For some, this cuts to the core of not just merely how we view ourselves considering the loss event, but how this loss shapes or re-shapes our very identity. Connecting to others, such as friends and family, helps us acknowledge our human need for community. Finally, connection at times will include reaching out to professionals for support, including during times of loss.

EXERCISE: WHO AM I?

Connection with others is embedded into our humanity, but what happens to us when connections are severed? Consider your identity and how it may have been impacted by the loss of a loved one or the end of that relationship. Whether this loss was due to a death, or a divorce, or something else that terminated or changed the relationship, how might the loss have altered how you view yourself and who you are?

Who was I before the person entered my life?

Who was I during my relationship with this person? Include ways in which you may have changed throughout the relationship, including at the relationship's beginning, middle, and end.

Who am I now since this person is no longer in my life?

How has their departure from my life changed me?

EXERCISE: CHALLENGE FAULTY THINKING

Faulty thinking patterns, also known as cognitive distortions, are incorrect or false thinking habits that we have, and these faulty thoughts can include thoughts related to our losses. We will begin by challenging some of the faulty thinking we may have about how different genders express emotion. Have you ever heard anyone say, "Big boys don't cry" or, "Women are too emotional?" Think about some of the messages you have received (explicitly and implicitly) throughout your life that may have shaped the way you express or do not express your true emotions. Describe these messages, identify where the message came from (e.g., parents, peers, culture, music, social media, movies, etc.), and include whether these messages have been healthy or unhealthy for you.

Messages I've Learned About Expressing Emotions	Where Did the Message Come From?	Was the Message Healthy or Unhealthy for Me?

Figure 14: Challenge Faulty Thinking

S&C

A

EXERCISE: WHAT ARE MY GRIEF SYMPTOMS?

Do you know your personal symptoms of grief? Below, begin to list what you think are your grief symptoms. Consider grief's impact from a bio-psycho-social-spiritual (biological, psychological, social, and spiritual) perspective. (As an aside, I note here this term is commonly written as biopsychosocial-spiritual, however, I elect to separate each word to emphasize its components.) Include how grief may be impacting you physically (headaches, stomachaches, etc.), emotionally (sadness, crying, anger, etc.), mentally (constant thoughts about the loss event, etc.), socially (loss of friends, difficulties at work, etc.), and spiritually (has your loss event/events caused you to question your belief systems, including spirituality?).

Do you think grief symptoms are different due to gender differences? Why or why not? List ways in which grief symptoms have or have not been related to gender identity in your own experience.

&C

A

EXERCISE: TURNING DOWN THE GRIEF VOLUME

Loss enters our world and sometimes stays there. For many of us, a loss is something we never quite get over. Grief expert, Mary-Frances O'Connor, stated once in an interview: "The background is running all the time for people who are grieving."[83] This background of grief can be like a loud discordant noise and, at other times, a sweet soft melody.

Think of your grief as sounds or background music in your life. How do you hear (perceive) your grief now? Is it a loud and ever-pervasive part of your day? Or is it soft and in the background?

Is the "sound" of your daily grief experience mournful or painful? This can occur when you recall difficult details or parts of your loss narrative that are painful.

Does the "sound" of your grief also include times when it is like a sweet melody that lifts you? This may happen, for example, when remembering something nice or fun about someone we lost.

Do you need to turn down your "grief volume" in your daily life? This can begin by creating a balance between time spent grieving and time doing other things that provide healthy and needed distractions. In what ways may you need to create more balance?

---

83 McCoy, 2021

EXERCISE:
MY LOSS STORYLINE

In this storyline today, describe a different loss than you addressed previously. Or, if you want to address the same loss, describe a different aspect of that loss. For example, if the primary loss you want to discuss is about the death of a loved one, today begin to address some of the secondary losses that followed. Secondary losses are those losses that occur as a result of the primary loss.

Primary And Secondary Losses: Example

An example of primary loss is Julie experiencing the death of her husband Peter. After Peter's death, Julie found herself struggling not only with Pete's passing (primary loss), but now also with having to handle so many things without him (secondary losses), like family finances, house chores, taking care of their children, etc. These examples of secondary losses include the many things Julie struggled to do without the support of Peter. Both primary and secondary losses have an impact on us, including our behaviors (actions) and feelings.

Using the template provided, on the top section list at least four secondary losses you have experienced after a primary loss. On the bottom section, briefly describe how each of those four secondary losses made you feel. An example is provided.

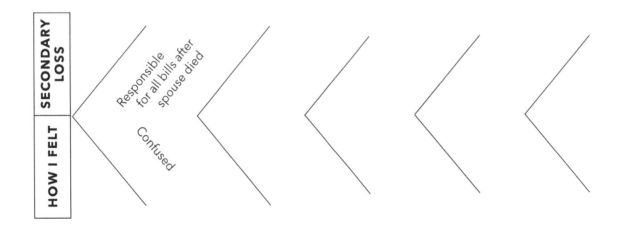

EXERCISE: JOURNALING TO EXPLORE MEMORIES AND EMOTIONS

Journaling can be a very useful tool to support grief work. We will begin here by journaling first about your memories and next about your feelings. In both journal prompts, write about a person (use the same person) with whom you had a significant relationship but now that relationship has ended. Perhaps the loss was due to a death, a separation/divorce, or some other event.

Note: If any feelings or thoughts become too difficult or overwhelming, pause this exercise and share this information with a mental healthcare professional.

Journaling Memories

Journal Prompt #1: What I remember most about this person is…

Journaling Feelings

Journal Prompt #2: What I feel about this person and this relationship is…

EXERCISE: BEHAVIOR ACTIVATION: ENGAGING IN HEALTHY ACTIVITIES

Behavior activation is the process of engaging in adaptive favorable activities, which helps minimize negative feelings and can replace unhealthy behaviors with healthy behaviors. Along the grief journey, we may have adopted some unhealthy activities (e.g., isolating, drinking too much, spending all day on the couch, etc.) that need to be replaced with healthier activities (e.g., taking a walk, visiting a friend, etc.).

What unhealthy activities have you been using to cope with your grief?

List ways you could replace those unhealthy activities with healthy ones.

Examples of healthy activities include:

Go for a walk	Visit a museum
Call a friend	Watch T.V.
Visit a family member	Draw, create art
Listen to music	Read a book
Take a bath	Exercise
Get a massage	Meditate or pray
Write in a journal	Go to the movies
Ride a bike	Pet an animal

 Chapter 7

ENGAGE IN THE NEW NORMAL

Topic: Engage in your new normal within a livable pattern of grief work

Exercises & Tools

- Creating the "New Normal"
- Bio-Psycho-Social-Spiritual Gaps
- Cognitive Journaling & Behavioral Journaling
- Problem-Solving
- Gratitude Journaling
- Visualization
- What Are You Focusing On?

MOVING INTO THE LIGHT: FINDING THE NEW NORMAL

The grieving process is something that has no set time limits and no clear end-line. Inasmuch as grieving provides us a mechanism for healing from losses big and small, grief remains ever present in one form or another, whether we are currently grieving a loss or anticipating some loss to come. Grieving is the process of healing from loss that we should invite into our everyday life. Since grief work is that mechanism for how we heal from our losses, why wouldn't we want this grief process to remain with us, healing and helping us our whole lives? We should create a space for grief and invite it into our homes and into our hearts.

Grieving is a cyclical process that ebbs and flows throughout all our lives. We do not one day magically stop grieving, so how do we move forward? We move forward *alongside* grief, in partnership with this amazing process for healing. Our final step in the grief process involves engaging in a "new normal" following a loss event. This new normal life will also include adopting a livable pattern on grief work into its flow. One way to achieve this is by utilizing the framework of the bio-psycho-social-spiritual model of care.

CONSTRUCTING A NEW NORMAL: THE BIO-PSYCHO-SOCIAL-SPIRITUAL FRAMEWORK

The bio-psycho-social-spiritual framework, incorporated into the GRACE Grief Model, is an important paradigm that can help us craft a new normal and construct a livable pattern of grieving that folds into our life in adaptive ways. Grief affects a person's cognitive, emotional, and behavioral responses,[84] and these responses can influence the bio-psycho-social-spiritual framework of a person (their biology, psychology, social interactions, and spirituality).

---

84 Shear et al., 2011

EXERCISE: CREATING THE "NEW NORMAL"

With a working appreciation that our loss experience impacts us biologically, psychologically, socially, and spiritually, we can build upon these domains as a stepping stone towards healing. Loss will always be part of our human condition, as will grief. A healthly life is one that acknowledges these truths and invites a healthy grieving process into the pattern of our day-to-day. After all, grieving is how we heal from loss. Borrowing from the many lessons and skills you have learned throughout this book, take the next step in your grief journey, which is to costruct your "new normal" framework. For this exercise, considering the following:

Biology: Your Physical Health

How has grief impacted you physically?

Are there any ways that grief has improved your physical self?

What steps are you willing to take to help address any negative or unhealthy impacts that grief may have caused you physically?

Psychology: Your Mental Health

How has grief impacted you psychologically?

Are there any ways grief has improved your mental self?

What steps are you willing to take to address any negative or unhealthy impacts grief may have caused to your mental heatlh?

Social: Your Relationship Health

How has grief impacted your relationships? This includes relationships with family, friends, and others (e.g, co-workers, community members, etc.)?

Are there any ways grief has improved your relationships?

What steps are you willing to take to address any negative or unhealthy impacts grief may have had on your relationships?

Spirituality: Your Spiritual Health

How has grief impacted you spiritually?

Are there any ways grief has improved your spiritual self?

What steps are you willing to take to address any negative or unhealthy impacts grief may have had on you spirituality?

EXERCISE: BIO-PSYCHO-SOCIAL-SPIRITUAL GAPS

The bio-psycho-social-spiritual model of care is a holistic paradigm for healing that allows the inclusion of key life areas: biology (your physical body), psychology (your mental health), social (your relationships and interactions with others), and spiritual (your spiritual self).

Considering the bio-psycho-social-spiritual model, in which of the four areas might you need to devote more attention?

How can you improve these identified gaps and improve your overall health?

Which exercises, tools, and techniques might you add or increase to help you?

EXERCISE: COGNITIVE JOURNALING & BEHAVIORAL JOURNALING

Two ways to encourage grief healing include journaling about cognitions (our thoughts) and behaviors (our actions). Write here about your *thoughts* relating to how grief has impacted you biologically, psychologically, socially, and spiritually. After that, write about any unhealthy *behaviors* (actions) you may have as a result of grief that are impacting you biologically, psychologically, socially, and spiritually.

EXERCISE: PROBLEM-SOLVING

As we move through our grief journey, including learning to re-story our grief narrative, one potential impediment is the problems we may face. Having a technique for problem-solving is a helpful way to help us get unstuck when challenged (or even debilitated) by dilemmas. Even though you may normally be a great problem-solver, grief has a way of making this process more difficult for many of us. Using a problem-solving guide or template, especially during times of grief, can prove very helpful for most people.

1. Identify the problem.

2. List any prior ways you have tried to solve this problem. Since these did not work, consider why these options were not successful.

3. List potential new solutions for addressing this problem.

4. Consider the pros and cons of each new potential solution.

5. Select the one solution that you believe is most ideal for addressing your problem at this time.

6. Try your new solution.

7. After trying the new solution, evaluate its success.

8. If it failed, consider why it may have failed. What might you need to change? Return to step #3 and re-create and re-evaluate a new list of potential solutions, then proceed again through steps #4–8 as needed. If you continue to struggle, reaching out to a trusted family member, friend, or seeking professional support may be needed.

EXERCISE: GRATITUDE JOURNALING

Another type of journaling that can be incredibly helpful in processing grief and balancing the emotions associated with loss is a gratitude journal. Being aware of what we have to be grateful for is more than a feel-good exercise, it can improve how we mentally feel. Gratitude interventions, such as gratitude journaling, improve psychological well-being.[85] Begin this exercise by naming and thinking about some of the people and things in your life for which you are grateful.

Who in the scope of my life am I grateful for? Why am I grateful for them?

Who has recently helped me in a big or small way? How have they helped me?

What in my life am I grateful for? Why am I grateful for this?

---

85   Boggiss et al., 2020

EXERCISE: VISUALIZATION

Visualization is a helpful relaxation technique. To begin, find a quiet safe place and sit with your eyes closed. Calm your breathing and relax your muscles (you may want to consider beginning with breath work and/or progressive muscle relaxation). Now form a mental image of something you find calming or peaceful that is both positive and in the present. Include as many details to support the image as possible.

What is the image you see? Describe what this image looks like. Does your image have any smells or sounds associated with it? If you could touch or physically feel what is in the image, how does that feel? What emotions or thoughts are evoked as you visualize this image?

EXERCISE: WHAT ARE YOU FOCUSING ON?

Painting by Buddy Turk

In your personal grief journey, what aspect(s) of your grief are you focusing on? Look at the painting above. Within the composition of shadowed trees, structures, and landscape, notice the solitary white-capped tree in the middle. This tree centers the artwork and provides a focal point. Using the grief coping techniques and tools learned in this book can help center you and provide a focal point, helping you navigate a way forward on your grief journey.

We have learned and practiced many tools and techniques but moving forward will also require us to focus on the right things, and focusing on healthy grief coping tools and techniques is the place to start.

What aspect(s) of your loss are you currently focusing on?

Do you need to shift your focus? What might you need to focus on to help you to move forward in the grieving process?

Which grief tools and exercises, including those in this workbook, might you include in your grief journey to promote healing and well-being?

 Chapter 8

LEAVING THE HARBOR: A FINAL WORD

Topic: Moving forward on your grief journey

Exercises & Tools

- My Grief Narrative Today
- Sharing My Grief Story
- Remembering & Celebrating Events
- My Personal Grief Model 2.0
- My Personal Grief Plan 2.0
- Acknowledging Progress
- Certificate of Grief Work Progression

LEAVING THE HARBOR

How tempting it may feel at times for us to remain where we are in the grieving process and not move forward. This, however, can keep us stuck in grief, stuck in an imagined safe harbor where we are lulled into believing familiar feelings of grief are comfortable and normal, creating for us a false sense of safety in which we fail to progress. "A ship in harbor is safe, but that is not what ships are built for."[86] Truly healing from loss often requires that we allow ourselves to leave perceived comfort areas, encouraging ourselves to be authentically and appropriately vulnerable in processing loss narratives. To heal, one must venture into the difficult waters of grief work, learning to live in a new normal while also allowing ourselves to continue being healed and re-healed by the grief processes. This healing process includes telling and re-telling our loss story, incorporating how

---

86 Shedd, 1928

we connect to ourselves and to others in this world and integrating elements of our personalized bio-psycho-social-spiritual paradigm.

YOUR GRIEF NARRATIVE

For the following exercise you will need two different color pens. To begin, write your grief story on the following page using one of the pens. Your writing should summarize where you are in your personal grief story at this time. Include details about your thoughts, feelings, and behaviors. Next, using the different color pen, add to this story with a focus on healing and creating a hopeful future. What new perspectives may be needed to help you move forward (new ways of thinking)? What new ways of doing things might you need to include to help support your healing (new behaviors, new actions)?

EXERCISE: MY GRIEF NARRATIVE TODAY

You will need two different-colored pens for this exercise. Continue on additional lined paper as needed. See the previous page for instructions.

EXERCISE: SHARING MY GRIEF STORY

Some of you may be ready at this time to begin sharing your grief stories with others. Sharing our stories can allow us to move forward in our own healing journeys, as well as provide others with the hope and support that they may need to move toward healthier ways of coping with loss.

If you are ready and willing to share parts of your grief journey with others, consider taking these steps:

1. What loss event (or events) am I willing and ready to talk about with others?

2. Who am I willing and ready to share this with?

3. When might I be ready to share? Am I ready now?

4. Are there any aspects of my loss story I am not willing or ready to share yet? If so, what are they?

5. How might sharing with others help me progress in my grief journey?

6. How might sharing with others help them deal with loss in healthier ways?

EXERCISE: REMEMBERING & CELEBRATING EVENT

Along your grief journey, it can be beneficial to acknowledge the successes you have made moving forward in your grieving process. At some point in your future (perhaps even now), you may benefit from acknowledgment of these accomplishments by marking the event. You can mark the event by both acknowledging the loss and, in cases of bereavement, honoring the deceased, as well as celebrating personal healing. This is not an either/or activity; it is a both/and event. Living in the "both/and" reality of remembering and dealing with the pain of the loss while at the same time allowing ourselves to heal and move forward into a new healthy normal is important to moving us towards our new hopeful story of healing.

An example of this type of event could include inviting close friends and family to both honor a deceased loved one by sharing photographs and stories of them, while also enjoying a celebratory cake acknowledging how you (and perhaps others) have moved forward from feelings of hopelessness to feelings of hope.

Are you ready for a Remembering & Celebrating Event? Why or why not?

If you are not ready for this celebration, what might need to occur in order for you to be ready?

If you are ready, how might you celebrate? When and where might you celebrate? Who else would you possibly involve in the planning or invite to this celebration?

What steps can you take today to make this celebration a reality at some point in your future?

EXERCISE: MY PERSONAL GRIEF MODEL 2.0

As we have learned in this book, for a healthy grief journey, we need healthy tools and techniques to support our healing process. In Chapter 2, you first examined your personal grief model (see page 37). It is time now to re-examine the model you created and, after having learned and practiced new healthier ways of grieving, re-create here your updated personal grief model. Complete the form below by filling in as much information and detail as you can. This grief model will help you create your new grief plan (see following exercise).

HOW I NOW GRIEVE	WHO OR WHAT TAUGHT ME TO GRIEVE THIS WAY?	IS THIS HEALTHY OR UNHEALTHY FOR ME?

A

EXERCISE: MY PERSONAL GRIEF PLAN 2.0

Today's Date:_____

I will continue to allow the process of grief to help me heal and grow.

I will remove *unhealthy* grief tools and techniques from my life (e.g., substance abuse, isolating, etc.). List the unhealthy grief tools and techniques you have been using that you want/need to stop:

I will incorporate the *healthy* grief tools and techniques I have learned. List the healthy grief tools and techniques you plan to use going forward:

I understand some thoughts around a loss event can be unhealthy. I will continue to work on improving my GRACE Grief Model Grief Map to allow me to understand more fully my loss, make sense of the loss, heal and move forward with my life in healthy ways.

EXERCISE: ACKNOWLEDGING YOUR PROGRESS

Complete and save the certificate on the next page to mark the progress you have made in your grief journey. Remember, grief is good because *grief is how we heal from loss,* so invite healthy grieving into your life. When you have finished your readings and the assignments within both the *GRACE: A Model for Grieving* handbook and this *GRACE: A Model for Grieving Workbook,* you will have achieved a tremendous amount of grief work.

The GRACE Grief Model supports:

- Deeper awareness of grief and loss (types of grief, impacts of grief, bio-psycho-social-spiritual impact of grief, meaning making/spiritual impacts, mapping your grief journey).

- Understanding grief as good, going to ebb and flow (cyclical), and a gift.

- Appreciating grief and culture.

- Allowing yourself to incorporate unique meaning making (spirituality) into your grief work.

- Learning and practicing many exercises and tools to support adaptive healing from loss.

- Allowing yourself to move forward in healthy ways after loss.

✳ HEALING THROUGH MY GRIEF JOURNEY

CERTIFICATE OF GRIEF WORK PROGRESSION

Acknowledging your progress and marking the successful completion of this book can be an important way to affirm your healthy grieving process as you journey forward.

On this date _____, I _____
celebrate my forward progress in my grief journey. As part of this journey, I have successfully completed the *GRACE: A Model for Grieving* handbook and the accompanying *GRACE: A Model for Grieving Workbook*. I also affirm:

- Grief is a journey that takes time. I will be patient with myself, as healing takes time. I will remember that slow progress is still progress.

- Grief is good because, when we grieve in healthy ways, grief is how we heal from loss. Therefore, I commit to embracing healthy ways to grieve and I invite the grieving process into my life today and every day.

- Grief is cyclical and I acknowledge that grief will ebb and flow.

- Grief is a gift because, as we grieve in healthy ways, grief allows me to grow as I heal from loss.

- I will allow myself to continue writing my loss stories and also remember to re-write them as needed (enriching the narratives to include fuller, honest, and accurate descriptions, including positive aspects that allow me to move forward and heal).

- I am now and will continue to move forward in my grieving process. I give myself full permission to heal.

- I will continue to allow others to support and help me on my journey. I affirm that we are created to heal, including grieving, in community.

- I am healing! I understand the reality of loss never goes away, but that my understanding can grow, and my painful feelings can heal. I will continue to move forward with renewed understanding and towards my hopeful future story.

ACKNOWLEDGEMENTS

IN ADDITION TO THANKING my husband Kirk and sons Ryan and Davis for their ongoing love and support, I express my deepest appreciation to these family members and friends whose imprint on my life shaped me as a youth and young adult, guiding me towards my call into the ministry of counseling.

Thank you sincerely to Keller and Jo Lynn Towns, Carl and Kathie Strickler, Buddy and Cathy Turk, COL (R) Ralph and Barbara Reece, Vice Admiral Johnny Wolfe Jr., Tammy and Larry Hernandez, Claudette Gallaway Jordan and the Gallaway family, David Maske, the late Roland Hicks, Kim Rankin Nicholson, Lynnette Trapp Thornton, Sue Ann Kurz Smith, Kathy Ellison, the late Pastor Chet Duft, Judy and Teresa Bell and the Bell Family, and Charlotte Knight Woisin and the Knight family.

✱ ABOUT THE AUTHOR

Dr. Kay Towns, DPC, LPC, is a licensed professional counselor and mental health advocate. She earned her doctorate in Professional Counseling from Mississippi College, a master's degree in counseling from Houston Graduate School of Theology, and a master's degree in theological studies from Southern Methodist University. She completed her clinical training at one of the top psychiatric hospitals in the U.S., The Menninger Clinic in Houston, Texas. Kay is also an ordained minister in The United Methodist Church. Her therapeutic approach is to provide support and feedback to help people effectively address personal life challenges.

✳ REFERENCES

Altena, E. & Chen, I. & Daviaux, Y. & Ivers, H. & Philip, P. & Morin, C. (2017). How hyperarousal and sleep reactivity are represented in different adult age groups: Results from a large cohort study on insomnia. *Brain Sciences, 7.* Doi: 10.3390/brainsci7040041.

Alvarez, E. Puliafico, A. Leonte, K. & Albano, A. (2019). Psychotherapy for anxiety disorders in children and adolescents. *UpToDate.* Retrieved at https://www.uptodate.com/contents/psychotherapy-for-anxiety-disorders-in-children-and-adolescents.

American Psychiatric Association (2013). *Diagnostic and statistical manual of mental disorders* (5th ed.), Washington, DC.

American Psychiatric Association (2022) *Diagnostic and statistical manual of mental disorders*, 5th Edition, text revision. Doi: 10.1176/appi.books.9780890425787.

Boyes, A. (2013). Cognitive restructuring. *Psychology Today.* Retrieved at https://www.psychologytoday.com/us/blog/in-practice/201301/cognitive-restructuring.

Barley, N. (1997). *Dancing On the Grave: Encounters with Death.* Hatchette, UK: Abacus.

Betz, G., & Thorngren, J. M. (2006). Ambiguous loss and the family grieving process. *The Family Journal, 14*(4), 359–365. Doi: 10.1177/1066480706290052.

Boggiss, A.L., Consedine, N.S., Brenton-Peters, J.M., Hofman, P.L., & Serlachius, A.S. (2020) A systematic review of gratitude interventions: Effects on physical health and health behaviors. *Journal of Psychosomatic Research,*135. Doi: 10.1016/j.jpsychores.2020.110165.

Boss, P. (2016). The context and process of theory development: The story of ambiguous loss. *Journal of Family Theory & Review, 8*(269-286). Doi: 10.1111/jftr.12152.

Cleveland Clinic (2023). Diaphragmatic breathing. Retrieved at https://my.clevelandclinic.org/health/articles/9445-diaphragmatic-breathing.

Deng, Y., Chang, L., Yang, M., Huo, M., & Zhou, R. (2016). Gender differences in emotional response: Inconsistency between experience and expressivity. *PLoS ONE, 11*(6). Doi: 10.1371/journal.pone.0158666.

Delavechia, T.R., Velasquez, M.L., Duran, E.P., Matsumoto, L.S., & de Oliveira, I.R. (2016). Changing negative core beliefs with trial-based thought record *Arch Clin Psychiatry, 43*(2):31-33.

Doka, K. J. (Ed.). (1989). *Disenfranchised Grief: Recognizing Hidden Sorrow.* Lanham, MD: Lexington Books/D.C. Heath and Com.

Doran, G.T. (1981). "There's a S.M.A.R.T. way to write management goals and objectives." *Management Review.* 70(11):35-36.

Eckman, P. (1972). Universal and cultural differences in facial expression of emotion. *Proceedings of the Nebraska Symposium on Motivation, 19,* 207–284. Lincoln, NE: University of Nerbraska Press.

Enez, O. (2018). Complicated grief: Epidemiology, clinical features, assessment and diagnosis. *Current Approaches in Psychiatry, 10*(3), 269-279. Doi: 10.18863/pgy.358110.

Hamilton, I.J. (2016). Understanding grief and bereavement. *Br J Gen Pract.* Oct;66(651):523. Doi: 10.3399/bjgp16X687325.

Hill, C. (2018). *Meaning in Life: A Therapists Guide.* American Psychological Association.

Heelas, P. (1986). Emotion talk across cultures. In Harre, R. (ed.), *The Social Construction of Emotions,* Basil Blackwell(234–266).

Henningsen, Peter. (2018). Management of somatic symptom disorder. *Dialogues in Clinical Neuroscience, 20* (23-31). Doi: 10.31887/DCNS.2018.20.1/phenningsen.

Humberman, A. (Host). (2022, May 30). The science and process of healing from grief (Audio podcast). Stanford School of Medicine. Retrieved at https://hubermanlab.com/the-science-and-process-of-healing-from-grief/.

Ito, M., Nakajima, S., Fujisawa, D., Miyashita, M., Kim, Y., Shear, M.K., Ghesquiere, A., & Wall, M.M. (2012). Brief measure for screening complicated grief: Reliability and discriminant validity. *PLoS ONE, 7*(2), e31209. Doi: 10.1371/journal.pone.0031209.

Jacobson, E. (1938). *Progressive Relaxation.* University of Chicago Press, Chicago.

Kaczkurkin, A. N., & Foa, E. B. (2015). Cognitive-behavioral therapy for anxiety disorders: an update on the empirical evidence. *Dialogues in clinical neuroscience, 17*(3), 337–346.

Kersting, A., Brahler, E., Glaesmer, H., & Wagner, B. (2011). Prevalence of complicated grief in a representative population-based sample. *Journal of Affective Disorders, 131*(1-3), 339-343. Doi: 10.1016/j.jad.2010.11.032.

Knowles, L.M., Jovel, K.S., Mayer, C.M., Bottrill, K.C., Kaszniak. A.W., Sbarra, D.A., Lawrence, E.E., & O'Connor, M.F. (2021). A controlled trial of two mind-body interventions for grief in widows and widowers. *J Consult Clin Psychol.* 2021 Jul;89(7):640-654. Doi: 10.1037/ccp0000653. PMID: 34383536.

Lathrop D. (2017). Disenfranchised grief and physician burnout. *Ann Fam Med*. Jul;15(4):375-378. Doi: 10.1370/afm.2074.

Lim, N. (2016). Cultural differences in emotion: differences in emotional arousal level between the East and the West. *Integr Med Res*. Jun;5(2):105-109. Doi: 10.1016/j.imr.2016.03.004.

Linde, K., Treml, J., Steinig, J., Nagl, M., & Kersting, A. (2017). Grief interventions for people bereaved by suicide: A systematic review. *PLoS One*. Jun 23;12(6):e0179496. Doi: 10.1371/journal. pone.0179496.

Ma, X., Yue, Z.Q., Gong, Z.Q., Zhang, H., Duan, N.Y., Shi, Y.T., Wei. G.X., & Li, Y.F. The effect of diaphragmatic breathing on attention, negative affect and stress in healthy adults. *Front Psychol*. 2017 Jun 6;8:874. Doi: 10.3389/fpsyg.2017.00874.

McCoy, B. (2021, December 20). How your brain copes with grief, and why it takes time to heal. National Public Radio. Retrieved at https://www.npr.org/sections/health-shots/2021/12/20/1056741090/ grief-loss-holiday-brain-healing.

Miyabayashi, S., & Yasuda, J. (2007). Effects of loss from suicide, accidents, acute illness and chronic illness on bereaved spouse and parents in Japan: Their general health, depressive mood, and grief reaction. *Psychiatry and Clinical Neurosciences, 61*, 502-508. Doi: 10.1111/j.1440-1819.2007.01699.x.

Moayedoddin, B., & Markowitz, J.C. (2015). Abnormal grief: Should we consider a more patient-centered approach? *American Journal of Psychotherapy, 69*(4), 361-378.

Nakajima, S. (2018). Complicated grief: recent developments in diagnostic criteria and treatment. *Philosophical Transactions Royal Society B, 373*. Doi: 10.1098/rstb.2017.0273.

O'Connor, M.F., & Seeley, S.H. (2022). Grieving as a form of learning: Insights from neuroscience applied to grief and loss. *Curr Opin Psychol*. 2022 Feb;43:317-322. Doi: 10.1016/j.copsyc.2021.08.019. Epub 2021 Aug 20. PMID: 34520954; PMCID: PMC8858332.

Park, C.L. (2013). The meaning making model: A framework for understanding meaning, spirituality, and stress-related growth in health psychology. *The European Health Psychologist, 15*(2), 40-45.

Park, C.L., Currier, J.I., & Slattery, J. (2017). *Trauma, meaning, and spirituality*. Washington, D.C.: American Psychological Association

Park, C. L., & Edmonson, D. (2011). Symposium at Israeli University, IDC Herzliya. Retrieved at http://portal.idc.ac.il/en/symposium/hspsp/2011/documents/cpark-edmondson11.pdf.

Park, C.L., & Halifax, R.J. (2011). Religion and spirituality in adjusting to bereavement: Grief as burden, grief as a gift. In R.A. Neimeyer, D.L, Harris, H.R. Winokeur, & G.F. Thornton (Eds.), *Grief and Bereavement in Contemporary Society*. Routledge.

Peterson, L. (2017). The science behind the art of storytelling. Harvard Business Publishing. Retrieved at https://www.harvardbusiness.org/the-science-behind-the-art-of-storytelling/.

Peña-Vargas, C.I., Armaiz-Pena, G.N., & Castro-Figueroa, E.M. (2021). A Biopsychosocial approach to grief, depression, and the role of emotional regulation. *Behavioral Sciences, 11*, 110. Doi: 10.3390/bs11080110.

Rosmarin, D. (2018). *Spirituality, Religion, and Cognitive-Behavioral Therapy*. New York, NY: Guildford Press.

Rosner R, Pfoh G, Kotoučová M. Treatment of complicated grief. *Eur J Psychotraumatol.* 2011;2. DOI: 10.3402/ejpt.v2i0.7995. Epub 2011 Nov 14. PMID: 22893810; PMCID: PMC3402114.

Scheff, T. (2015). What are emotions? A physical theory. *Review of General Psychology, 19*(4), 458-464. Doi: 10.1037/gpr0000058.

Shear, M. K. (2011). Bereavement and the DSM-5. *Omega: Journal of Death and Dying, 64* (101–118). Doi: 10.2190/OM.64.2.a.

Shear, K., Simon, N., Wall, M., Zisook, S., Neimeyer, R., Duan, N., Reynolds, C., Lebowitz, B., Sung, S., Ghesquiere, A., Gorscak, B., Clayton, P., Ito, M., Nakajima, S., Konishi, T., Melhem, N., Meer, K., Schiff, M., O'Connor, M., First, M., Sareen, J., Bolton, J., Skritskaya, N., Mancini, A.D., & Keshaviah, A. (2011). Complicated grief and related bereavement issues for the DSM-5. *Depression and Anxiety, 28*(2), 103–117. Doi:10.1002/da.20780.

Shedd, J. (1928). Salt from My Attic, The Mosher Press, Portland, Maine; cited in *The Yale Book of Quotations* (2006) ed. Fred R. Shapiro, p. 705; there are numerous variants of this expression.

Schneck, N., Tu, T., Haufe, S., Bonanno, G. Galfalvy, H., Ochsner, K. Mann, J. & Sajda, P. (2018). Ongoing Monitoring of Mindwandering in Avoidant Grief Through Cortico-Basal-Ganglia Interactions. *Social Cognitive and Affective Neuroscience,14*. Doi: 10.1093/scan/nsy114.

Schrijver, K., & Schrijver, I. (2015). *Living with the Stars: How the Human Body Is Connected to the Life Cycles of the Earth, the Planets, and the Stars*. Oxford, UK: Oxford Press.

Shott, S. (1979). Emotion and social life: A symbolic interactionist analysis. *American Journal of Sociology, 84*(6), 1317-1334. Doi: 10.1086/226936.

Simon, N.M. (2013). Treating complicated grief. *JAMA, 310*(4), 416-23.

Stelzer, E.M., Zhou, N., Maercker, A., O'Connor, M.F. & Killikelly, C. (2020) Prolonged grief disorder and the cultural crisis. *Front. Psychol,* 10:2982. Doi: 10.3389/fpsyg.2019.02982.

Thimm, J.C., & Holland, J.M. (2017). Early maladaptive schemas, meaning making, and complicated grief symptoms after bereavement. *International Journal of Stress Management, 24*(4), 347-367. Doi: 10.1037/str0000042.

Thompson, B.E., & Neimeyer, R.A. (2014). Thompson, B. E., & Neimeyer, R. A. (Eds.). (2014). Grief and the Expressive Arts: Practices for Creating Meaning. *OMEGA - Journal of Death and Dying, 72*, 362-365. Doi: 10.1177/0030222815598047.

Towns, K.B. (2024). *GRACE: A Model for Grieving.* Hatherleigh Press.

Torpy, J.M., Burke, A.E., & Golub, R.M. (2011). Panic disorder. *JAMA,* Mar 23;305(12), 1256. Doi: 10.1001/jama.305.12.1256. PMID: 21427380.

Tyler, J.M., & Darrow, N.T. (2022), The impact of cultural resiliency on traumatic loss, *Counseling Today*, January 2023, 40-45. Retrieved at https://ct.counseling.org/2023/01/the-impact-of-cultural-resiliency-on-traumatic-loss/.

Vesnaver E., Keller H.H., Sutherland O., Maitland S.B., & Locher J.L. (2016). Alone at the table: Food behavior and the loss of commensality in widowhood. *J Gerontol B Psychol Sci Soc Sci.* Nov. 71(6),1059-1069. Doi: 10.1093/geronb/gbv103.

White, M. (2007). *Maps of narrative practice.* New York, NY: Norton.

White, M., & Epston, D. (1990). *Narrative means to therapeutic ends.* New York, NY: Norton.

Williams-Reade, J., Freitas, C., & Lawson, L. (2014). Narrative-informed medical family therapy: Using narrative therapy practices in brief medical encounters. *Families, Systems, & Health, 32*(4), 416-425. Doi: 10.1037/fsh0000082.

Wortmann, J.H., & Park, C.L. (2009). Religion/spirituality and change in meaning after bereavement: Qualitative evidence for the meaning making model. *Journal of Loss and Trauma, 14*(1), 17-34. Doi: 10.1080/15325020802173787.